# SECRETS OF THE I CHING

AF663856

DR. JOSEPH MURPHY

PARKER

PUBLISHING COMPANY

parkerpub.co

All rights reserved. No part of this publication may be reproduced, stored in a retrieval system, or transmitted in any form or by any means, electronic, mechanical, photocopying or otherwise, without the prior permission of the copyright owner.

The views and ideas expressed in this book are the personal opinions of the author, and do not necessarily represent the views of the Publisher.

© Copyright 1970 by Parker Publishing Company

**www.parkerpub.co**

*Previous Books by the Author:*

Amazing Laws of Cosmic Mind Power
Infinite Power for Richer Living
Miracle of Mind Dynamics
The Cosmic Power Within You
The Power of Your Subconscious Mind
Your Infinite Power to Be Rich

# Secrets of the I Ching

JOSEPH MURPHY

D.D., D.R.S., Ph.D., LL.D.

Fellow of the Andhra Research
University, India

PARKER PUBLISHING COMPANY, INC.
West Nyack, N.Y.

## *FOREWORD*

The *I Ching, or Book of Changes,* Third Edition, The Richard Wilhelm translation from Chinese into German, rendered into English by Cary F. Baynes, with a Foreword by C. G. Jung, and a Foreword to the new edition by Hellmut Wilhelm, Bollingen Series XIX, Princeton University Press, is the one I use and recommend that you use in connection with this book. I suggest you read the marvelous and most interesting Foreword by the late world-famous psychiatrist C. G. Jung of Zurich, in the Wilhelm/Baynes book just recommended. You will find it to be an introduction to the insight and wonders of the *I Ching.*

# What This Book Can Do For You

The unique feature of this book is its down-to-earth practicality. Here you are presented with simple, usable techniques and formulas of *I Ching* which you can easily apply for your day-to-day questions and problems for true guidance.

I have taught the simple processes incorporated in this book of *I Ching* in many classes to men and women of all professions and occupations. Many people came from distances up to a hundred miles for each class. The special features of this book show the interaction and working of the conscious and subconscious mind and the results that accordingly take place. The *I Ching* deals with the mystic process of the male and female principle within all of us, and whenever a person gets a particular *I Ching* Hexagram in answer to his or her question, the answer is given in simple, psychological, but understandable language. For those who are Biblically oriented, the answer is given in Biblical terminology to a no less understandable degree.

*Secrets of the I Ching* reveals the art of using the miracle-working powers of your deeper subconscious mind. The great eternal truths and principles of your mind antedate all religions or philosophy. The ancient and infallible wisdom contained in *I Ching* existed before any church or world came into being. In other words, it is eternal, but completely applicable for any answer you ask of it as will be shown in this book.

It is with these thoughts in mind that I urge you in the following chapters to use this wonderful, magical transforming Power which will aid and assist you, guide and direct you, solve your problems, attain the objects of your desires, free the fear-ridden mind, and liberate you completely from lack, limitation, and frustration of all kinds. All you have to do in order to get an answer to any particular question is throw the coins, as directed, six times, thereby activating the infallible powers of your deeper mind.

Remember, the infinite intelligence and boundless wisdom resident in your subconscious mind is all-wise, knows all, and sees all, and you are simply using an ancient but simple mathematical process of receiving a true answer.

Begin now, today. Let wonders happen in your life through the guidance of *I Ching* that you may not have thought possible previously.

JOSEPH MURPHY

# *Contents*

# 1

# The Book of Changes and What It Can Bring to You

The *Book of Changes* is full of mystic sayings and seemingly abstruse matter of a symbolic nature. It is said that Confucius was seventy years old when he first took up the study of the *Book of Changes* called *I Ching* (pronounced Yee Jing). The wisdom contained in the *I Ching* goes back about 5,000 years. Lao-tze, the famous Chinese mystic, was a profound student of the *I Ching* and many of his famous aphoristic sayings were culled from the eternal verities expounded in this age-old book of wisdom, truth and beauty. It is a book of incredible antiquity, and some of the most profound thinkers in the world have been avid readers and students of its contents.

### *Sixty-Four Hexagrams*

This book is based on sixty-four hexagrams; that is, sixty-four six-line figures, each figure or complex being composed of undivided and divided lines. These hexagrams reveal what the book has to say. The judgments in each hexagram sum up your present subconscious state of mind and your outer circumstances together with the outcome you may expect. The images reveal the symbolic meaning of the lines in the hexagram and point out their application to your present personal, social, business or worldly situation.

### *Wilhelm/Baynes Edition of I Ching*

The *I Ching*, or *Book of Changes*, Third Edition, The Richard Wilhelm translation from Chinese into German, rendered into English by Cary F. Baynes, with a foreword by the late Professor Carl G. Jung, of Zurich, Switzerland, and a foreword to the new edition by Hellmut Wilhelm, Bollingen Series XIX, Princeton University Press, is the one I use and recommend that you use in connection with this book. I suggest you read the marvelous and most interesting foreword by the late world-famous psychiatrist Carl Jung in the Wilhelm/Baynes book just recommended. You will find it to be an introduction to the insight and wonders of the *I Ching*.

### *The Way I Ching Works*

Hellmut Wilhelm, the famous German scholar, who studied with a Chinese sage and who is today an outstanding authority on the hidden wisdom of the *I Ching*, explains the use of the book as follows: "The way in which the *Book of Changes* works can best be compared to an electrical circuit reaching into all situations. The circuit only affords the potentiality of lighting; it does not give light. But when contact with a definite situation is established through the questioner, the 'current' is activated and the given situation is illumined."* This is a simple explanation of the way it works.

### *Principle of Constant Change*

The Chinese mystics who wrote the *I Ching* were past masters in the art of psychology, and they intuitively perceived the laws underlying the cosmos and the society of man. They accepted the opposites

*Book 2, page 315. Permission granted by Princeton University Press.

in this world and the principle of constant change. Action and reaction are constant in the cosmos. There are ups and downs, night and day, rain and sunshine, hot and cold, male and female, conscious and subconscious, ins and outs, sweet and sour, good and evil, pains and pleasures, sadness and joy.

The *I Ching* points out how you can establish peace of mind and an inner harmony by tuning in on the Infinite Being within you and thereby bringing about serenity and equilibrium in your life.

The *Book of Changes* reveals to you that everything passes. Nothing is forever. It teaches you to go back to the "center," where Tao, or God, dwells and to establish yourself in harmony with God; then you will reconcile the opposites in your life. When poised, serene, calm and quiet in the presence of God, you can decide how to handle any situation.

### *Time and Its Importance*

There is a time for everything under the sun. There is a time to sow and a time to reap. There is a time to work and a time for rest. There is a time to act and a time to remain still and quiet. Time is also psychological: it is a state of consciousness. It is your thought, your feeling, your awareness. When there is confusion, resentment and hostility in your subconscious, the hexagram points out to you that it is the wrong time to make a decision and that your attitude will bring loss and failure.

### *How Do I Get Out of Danger or My Dilemma?*

The *I Ching* is not a book of fortune-telling. You will learn later in this book how to consult the *I Ching*, a procedure which enables you to activate the spiritual powers of your subconscious mind. When you request an answer from the *I Ching*, you must take it seriously. Be honest and sincere, and maintain a healthy reverence for the Divinity which shapes your end. You are consulting the wisdom of the ages. *I Ching* teaches you to establish harmony in the "center," and you will have good fortune. You can pour out God's river of peace on the troubled waters of life. All opposites change to their own opposites. When you remain in tune with the Infinite, no change can really disturb you.

## *Your Next Move*

A relative of mine whose daughter was missing for twelve months consulted the *I Ching* and received Hexagram 5. Symbolically and intuitively she knew what was meant when it told her it would be advantageous to cross the great sea. After consulting the *I Ching* she had a dream which showed her where her daughter was staying in London, England. She immediately went by plane and rescued her daughter from what undoubtedly would have been a certain death, morally and psychologically, as well as physically.

The *I Ching* tells you about your present state of mind or that of another, and understanding that, you evolve the solution of your "next move." *I Ching* does not give specific direction; it talks about you. Reading this and interpreting "you," makes it possible for you to establish harmony and unity in the Secret Place of the Most High within you, when all will be well.

## *The Most Popular Technique in Consulting the I Ching*

The most popular and practical method used by students of the *I Ching* consists in the throwing of three coins, pennies for example, or dimes or nickels, a total of six times, recording tails or heads for each throw. Some say you should use yarrow stalks. In reality, it makes no difference, as the whole procedure depends on your receptive attitude of mind. When you realize that all you are doing is activating the wisdom of your subconscious, and that when you are passive, receptive, and have a healthy respect for the Infinite Intelligence resident in your subconscious mind, knowing that It alone knows the answer, it makes no difference whether you use pennies, yarrow stalks or Chinese coins with a hole in the center.

You are using a mechanical approach to tapping the spiritual agencies within your subconscious depths. You could say you were contacting your Higher Self, your Superconscious, your Subliminal Self or Infinite Intelligence. All this verbalism leads nowhere. It is sufficient to know that in your subconscious depths* is the answer to all the problems under the sun.

*See *The Power of Your Subconscious Mind*, by Dr. Joseph Murphy, Prentice-Hall, Inc., Englewood Cliffs, New Jersey, 1963.

*Why This Book*

A few months ago I conducted a class before a wonderful group of men and women of all ages and professions. I explained many of the meanings in the light of the Bible and our knowledge of mental and spiritual laws. Men and women, bankers, doctors, legal secretaries, real estate men, actors and actresses asked questions at these nightly sessions, and all agreed that the hexagrams they received were most appropriate and highly relevant to their particular problem. One real estate investor saved over $100,000 by asking a question: "Should I invest in this real estate proposition which is presented to me?" The answer was a resounding "No."

This book is intended for the layman, the man in the street, the housewife, the stenographer, the salesman, the department store buyer, the pharmacist, the taxi driver and the busy executive. It is in no way intended to take the place of the most excellent of all books on the *I Ching*, the Wilhelm/Baynes Edition already recommended in this chapter.

I am not going into the highly technical, mathematical, allegorical, figurative and mystical lore of the book. All I wish to do here is to try to transmit all this mysticism and Oriental symbolism to the understanding of the "common people," so that when you look up my comments on each hexagram you may find simple Bible truths with which you are familiar and their psychological application for your everyday living. The overriding theme of this book is its practicality, simplicity, and case histories to illustrate how you may get answers to aid in solving problems. Furthermore, you will have the great joy of developing your intuitive faculties so that ofttimes you may get spontaneous flashes of intuitive illumination which correspond exactly and in minute detail with the hexagram you received appertaining to the same situation.

Climb the Oriental ladder of wisdom and move onward, upward and Godward.

*POINTS TO REMEMBER*

1. The *Book of Changes* is full of mystic sayings and abstract matter of a symbolic nature. It was a book studied by Confucius

and Lao-tze and many of their aphoristic sayings are attributed to the *I Ching*.

2. A hexagram is a six-line figure composed of divided and undivided lines. They reveal your present mental attitude and subconscious beliefs.
3. The way the *I Ching* works is likened to an electrical circuit. The circuit is the potential lighting; it does not give light. When contact with a definite situation is established through your question, you can activate the spiritual power of your subconscious mind and the answer comes. Light means the Supreme Intelligence resident in your subconscious mind.
4. The *I Ching* points out that you can establish peace and harmony in your life by tuning in on the Infinite Being called Tao (God) and letting the harmony and love of God direct you.
5. The *I Ching* points out that in this objective, three-dimensional world there is a time and place for everything. There is a time to sow and a time to reap. There is a time to work and rest. When confused, it is the wrong psychological time to make a decision or act.
6. The *I Ching* is not a book of fortune-telling. In this volume you are consulting the wisdom of the ages, going back over 5,000 years. *I Ching* teaches you to establish harmony at the Center of your Being, and all your ways will be pleasantness and all your paths will be peace.
7. The *I Ching* tells you about your present state of mind or that of another, and understanding that, you evolve the solution of your "next move."
8. The most popular method of consulting the *I Ching* is through the tossing of coins, and as you become sincere, receptive, passive and feel and know what you are doing, your subconscious will present you with the appropriate hexagram.
9. You are simply using a mechanical approach to tapping the spiritual power of your subconscious mind.
10. This present book is intended for the man in the street free from mystical, metaphysical and allegorical phraseology so that you can understand the answers when you ask a question. This book is for you.

# 2

# The Eight Basic Trigrams in the I Ching

A brief survey of these eight symbols that form the basis of the *Book of Changes* yields the following classification:*

| | | *Name* | *Attribute* | *Image* | *Family Relationship* |
|---|---|---|---|---|---|
| ☰ | Ch'ien | the Creative | Strong | Heaven | Father |

*Reprinted by permission of Princeton University Press.

| | *Name* | | *Attribute* | *Image* | *Family Relationship* |
|---|---|---|---|---|---|
| ☷ | K'un | the Receptive | Devoted, yielding | Earth | Mother |
| ☳ | Chen | the Arousing | Inciting movement | Thunder | First son |
| ☵ | K'an | the Abysmal | Dangerous | Water | Second son |
| ☶ | Ken | Keeping Still | Resting | Mountain | Third son |
| ☴ | Sun | the Gentle | Penetrating | Wind, wood | First daughter |

| | | *Name* | *Attribute* | *Image* | *Family Relationship* |
|---|---|---|---|---|---|
| ☲ | Li | the Clinging | Light-giving | Fire | Second daughter |
| ☱ | Tui | the Joyous | Joyful | Lake | Third daughter |

## *Psychological Everyday Meaning of the Eight Trigrams*

*Ch'ien* and *K'un* represent your conscious and subconscious mind, the male and female principle in each of us. For example, the idea, aspiration, or desire you have, when emotionalized and felt as true, sinks into the subconscious mind where it dies and comes forth as an answer to your prayer. You could liken the process to an apple seed deposited in the ground, which undergoes a sort of metamorphosis and then comes forth as the apple tree with its fruit.

*Chen*, the Arousing, the first son (or idea) means your dominant idea, your desire, that which you wish to achieve.

*K'an*, the Abysmal, the second son, means your present limitation. Your thoughts come in pairs. The thought comes to you that you want guidance, a solution to a problem, and another thought comes to your mind, "There is no way out." The latter thought must die and the first must live. The negative thought (second son) dies when you realize there is an Infinite Intelligence within your subconscious mind that knows all and sees all and will respond to you.

*Ken*, Keeping Still, the third son, means you quiet the wheels of your mind, focus your attention on your goal, your desire, knowing there is an Almighty Power which responds to the focal point of your attention.

*Sun*, the Gentle, first daughter, means that as you remain focussed quietly and lovingly on your ideal and the spirit of God, the feeling of oneness will move over the waters of your mind giving you assurance your prayer will be answered.

*Li*, the Clinging, second daughter, means you persist in faith and confidence, an attitude of stick-to-itiveness and determination, knowing that he who perseveres to the end shall succeed. It also means loving the good, i.e., you are emotionally attached to that which is noble and God-like.

*Tui*, the Joyous, third daughter, represents the joy and satisfaction at the conclusion of an enterprise or assignment well done. The engineer similarly discovers the joy of overcoming a tough problem in building a bridge. The Bible says: . . . *The joy of the Lord is your strength* (Nehemiah 8:10). Having gone through these steps in prayer, you have succeeded in impregnating your subconscious mind and you experience the joy of the answered prayer.

## *Light and Dark Trigrams*

— — 6
—— 5
— — 4
—— 3
— — 2
—— 1

Light and dark trigrams represent male and female aspects of your mind. A trigram contains three lines. Two trigrams, or six lines, make a hexagram. Light means male and dark means female. The straight lines are male and the divided lines female. For example, in the hexagram you see on this page, the lines marked 1, 3 and 5 are light, or male, and the lines marked 2, 4 and 6 are dark, or female. Odd numbers are male and even numbers are female.

## *The Hexagram (6 Lines) and What It Means*

A hexagram consists of six lines, representing man. Man is composed of spirit, mind and body—there are different degrees of the same thing (Spirit). Using the analogy of ice, water and steam: These are all the same, only they have different degrees of vibration. Steam has a much higher molecular vibration than water. Water is used to drink, ice to preserve your food, and steam can be used to take the grease off your motor car. Each has a different function, yet they are all the same; namely, $H_2O$.

### *Spirit and Matter*

Matter is the lowest degree of spirit and spirit is the highest degree of matter. Once when the great Einstein was asked what matter was, he said it was energy reduced to the point of visibility. Energy is a scientific term for spirit.

### *The Hexagram and the Trinity*

The Chinese explain the Trinity by the picture of a father, mother and a child. When two things join together we have a third. When the father fertilizes the ovum of his wife, we acquire a son bearing witness of the father and mother. In simple, everyday psychological terms, your conscious mind is the father generating the idea or desire, your mother is the female aspect, your subconscious mind called the womb in the Bible, which means your receptive attitude of mind whereby you completely accept your desire. By enveloping it with feeling and enthusiasm, your desire will be embodied in your subconscious mind; and the answer to your prayer is the son, or the function, experience or event you desired. Your subconscious expresses whatever is impressed upon it.

### *The Six Lines and the Three-fold Man*

The two lower lines represent your body, environment, the world; the middle two lines represent man or mind; and the top two lines represent spirit. The word "body" represents not only your physical body, but your environment, condition, social status and all things appertaining to you on the three-dimensional plane. The word "man" means mind—in this instance your subconscious mind (the creative medium, the female aspect). Spirit represents your conscious mind; not that your conscious, reasoning mind is spotless, holy, pure and immaculate like Spirit, but from a functional standpoint your conscious mind is Spirit, because you have the capacity to choose, select and initiate something which you turn over to your subconscious mind, the great fabricator or builder which accepts it and embodies it on the screen of space.

### *Chinese Wisdom*

Lao-tze said: "From one comes two, from two comes three and from three the whole world." God is the Living Spirit Almighty, One and Indivisible. For the purposes of creation, God divides Himself into two, male and female, the father and mother principle. All things are made by the contemplation of Spirit. Spirit contemplates Itself as the sun, moon, stars, galaxies in space and all things therein contained and their images are reflected in the female aspect of Itself, which brings forth all things in the image and likeness of the male aspect. In other words, the male principle is called 1, the female 2, and from the union of these two comes 3, or the whole world. This is the way all things are made, and there is nothing made that is not made that way.

### *The Creative and Receptive*

These are the words used by *I Ching* to represent the father-mother principle, or God dividing Himself into two for the purposes of creation. The Chinese wisdom points out that the entire universe—animals, man plus the infinite galaxies of space—came forth from the interaction of these two principles. This is the real basis of the *I Ching* teaching.

### *Man Creates the Same Way*

You are made in the image and likeness of God. In other words, your spirit is God's spirit. Your mind is God's mind and the Life-Principle (God) in you flows through the matrix of your habitual thinking and imaging. Your world (body, condition, environment and experience) is the image and likeness of your inner beliefs and conditioning.

### *What the I Ching Teaches*

In simple psychological language, the essence of the *I Ching* teaching is that if your conscious and subconscious mind work together harmoniously, peacefully and synchronously in accordance with Divine ideas and the eternal verities, the children (results, experiences) from such a harmonious interaction will be health, happiness, peace, abundance and security. When the two phases of your mind work in concord, in accord and in unison, you will experience heaven on earth. Likewise, physically, when a husband and wife work together harmoniously, loving one another, and when each exalts God in the other, the marriage grows more blessed through the years. They prosper, are happy and succeed in all their undertakings; and their children reflect the love and harmony of their parents. This is why it is said, "Wisdom is justified of her children."

### *The Psychological Meaning of Six, Seven Eight and Nine Used in the Hexagrams*

Numbers in the Bible and in the *I Ching* represent attributes and potencies of God. For example, the numeral one is a symbol of God and is frequently referred to in the Bible. God, or One, is the origin of all things and the cause of all things.

Two is two units or two ones; four is four units, and so on. Two represents division, the opposites, such as male and female, night and day. Psychologically, two represents your desire. When you have a desire, your mind is divided; it is not in a state of wholeness or oneness. Nourish, sustain and give attention to your desire, feeling and knowing that as you meditate on it you will appropriate and assimilate it into your subconscious mind, where it will die.

Three means conviction, subconscious impregnation, where you no longer have the desire. This is a conditioned state which follows the work you did with Number 2.

Four represents the manifestation or the objectification of your subconscious impression. It is also a symbol of the world.

Five, representing the sum of 2 and 3, is the working of wisdom and understanding. Wisdom is the awareness of the Presence and Power of God within you, and understanding is the application of the God-Power in your everyday affairs. Five is also a symbol of imagination (disciplined). Whatever you imagine and feel to be true will come to pass.

Six, frequently used in the *I Ching*, is a symbol of the six-pointed star, which means the harmonious relationship of your conscious and subconscious mind. When these two agree on anything, your prayer is always answered. *Six days may work be done, but in the seventh is the Sabbath of rest holy to the Lord . . .* (Exodus 31:15). Psychologically speaking, six and sex are synonymous. Biblically and metaphysically speaking, six days do not refer to days of the week, but the length of time it takes you to impregnate or convey an idea or desire to your subconscious mind. When you claim and feel yourself to be what you want to be, or possess what you want to possess, and when you have succeeded in fixing that state in your subconscious mind, it is called the sixth day. You know when the sixth day comes because you no longer desire what you possess in your consciousness. This may take you a minute, an hour, a week or a month, depending on your spiritual growth and the nature of your request.

Seven is used frequently throughout the Bible. I shall only use a few references. Samson's strength was indicated by his seven locks of hair. *And on the seventh day God ended His work which He had made; and He rested on the seventh day from all His work which He had made* (Genesis 2:2). *And he stayed yet other seven days; and sent forth the dove; which returned not again unto him any more* (Genesis 8:12). The seventh day, the seventh hour, the seventh vial, the seven lamps, the seventh seal, the seven angels all mean the same thing.

Seven means a sense of oneness with God. It means Divine impregnation or the interval of time between impregnation of your subconscious and the resultant objective manifestation. This is also called the Sabbath, or seventh day, but in reality it has nothing to do with days of the week. Look at the number seven. It is two one's joined together, symbolizing your conviction of your good. Psychologically, the seventh day or Sabbath follows the six days of labor, which simply means a sense of rest follows your subjective acceptance of your desire. It is somewhat similar to a woman who is pregnant. She is careful and circumspect while carrying the child, and after a period of time she gives birth. Likewise, you know you are carrying a child (answered prayer) within you and in due time you will give birth to the answered prayer. Seven means hidden wisdom, rest, stillness, quiescence.

Eight. *And on the eighth day the flesh of his foreskin shall be circumcised* (Leviticus 12:3). *And they shall be eight boards* (Exodus 26:25. . . . *He reigned eight years in Jerusalem* (II Chronicles 21:5). The numeral eight appears numerous times in the Bible. It is a symbol of Infinity which has no beginning or end. Eight is the digit value of the name Jehovah (JHVH). The movement of the hand in writing the number eight is a rhythmic alternation which suggests action and reaction, involution and evolution. Eight means also splendor, fulness, greatness, immensity, infinity. Circumcision takes place on the eighth day. Psychologically, this means when you become aware of the truth that the "I Am" in you is God, i.e., pure Being, Life, Awareness; and as you tune in with the Infinite, knowing that the Life-Principle is the Father of all and that all men are your brothers, you will sense your oneness with all life and with all men throughout the world. As you claim that which is true of God is also true of you, you will go from glory to glory, and from octave to octave, which is symbolized by the numeral eight, which has no beginning or end. Eight means you are moving onward, upward and Godward. Circumcision on the eighth day is a mental and spiritual act. The moment you realize you are the tabernacle of the Living God and when you divest yourself of your name, nationality, social status and all things appertaining to your personality, you realize you are unveiling the God-Presence, which is the eighth day, or eighth hour, or eighth son, etc.

The number nine, as the last of the series of numeral symbols, represents completion, attainment, realization, the end of a cycle. Every end is the seed of a fresh beginning. *Nine cubits was the length thereof* . . . (Deuteronomy 3:11). *Over all the land until the ninth hour* (Matthew 27:45). . . . *The ninth hour Jesus cried* . . . (Matthew 27:46). . . . *And at the ninth hour I prayed* . . . (Acts 10:30). Psychologically speaking, nine means a new birth in God wherein your intellect is illumined from On High. A woman gives birth in the ninth month; likewise, you give birth to God's wisdom, truth and beauty, oftentimes attended by a mystic illumination. Nine means also fulfillment of a certain goal in your life, such as reaching the pinnacle of your profession in science, art or industry; but there is no end. When you have reached what you believe to be the top rung of the ladder, there is a new beginning, for there is no end to the glory which is man.

Ten is simply God magnified in your experience. Psychologically, and from a phallic standpoint, ten consists of one (male) and zero (female, womb), a symbol of God in action The *I Ching* points out that all creation in the universe is based on the interaction of the male and female principle of life.

### *Six, Seven, Eight and Nine*

You will notice that only these numbers appear on the hexagrams, as the Chinese mystics point out that all your experiences in life here can be expressed by the interaction of these numbers on the six lines.

You have sixty-four hexagrams. Six and four equal ten—the interaction of your conscious mind (1) and your subconscious mind (0). All the experiences and events of your life can be revealed through these sixty-four hexagrams. When you use a hexagram you are simply tapping the wisdom of your subconscious mind, which reveals to you the answer.

## *POINTS TO REMEMBER*

1. The eight trigrams represents the family comprising father, mother, three sons and three daughters and their relationship to one another. These eight trigrams, psychologically speaking, represent states of mind within you.
2. Light and dark trigrams represent the male and female aspects of your own mind. These are called Yang (male) and Yin (female) in Chinese terminology.
3. The six lines of a hexagram represent yourself—spirit, mind and body.
4. Spirit and matter are one and the same thing. Matter is spirit reduced to the point of visibility.
5. The trinity symbolizes a hexagram also. When your conscious and subconscious agree on anything, then there is an issue from

that union which is the expression of what is impressed upon your subconscious mind.

6. The two lower lines of the hexagram represent the body, the two middle lines the mind, and the two upper lines the spirit.
7. The Creative and Receptive represent the father-mother principle of life from which all things come forth. God, or Tao, divides Himself into two for the purposes of creation.
8. Man creates the same way as God creates. God imagines Himself to be something, and then God becomes that which He imagines Himself to be. Man has the same spirit and the same mind as God, and whatever man imagines himself to be and feels the reality of, it comes to pass in his life.
9. *I Ching* teaches that if your conscious and subconscious interact harmoniously, peacefully and joyfully, the result of this union will be wealth, happiness and the abundant life.
10. Numbers represent the attributes, qualities and potencies of God. They are symbolic of states of consciousness. Six means impregnation of your subconscious. Seven means stillness, rest, conviction, a period of mental pregnancy. Eight means splendor, spiritual growth and an absolute conviction that the "I Am" in you is God and your oneness with all men and all life. Nine is the end of a cycle—a new birth in God, a fresh beginning following an inner illumination. The above are the four numbers used in *I Ching*.
11. Sixty-four hexagrams add six and four to equal ten, which symbolically means the interaction of the male (1) and the female (0). All things in the world are brought forth from the interaction of these two aspects of God.
12. The Chinese multiplied the eight hexagrams by eight, getting sixty-four hexagrams, which reveal all possible psychological states of man and answer over 4,000 questions.

# 3

# Synchronicity: How Your Future Is in Your Mind Now

The late Professor Carl Jung, in his foreword to *I Ching* (Wilhelm/ Baynes Edition, Bollingen Series XIX, Princeton University Press) defines synchronicity as follows:

> . . . Synchronicity takes the coincidences of events in space and time as meaning something more than mere chance; namely, a peculiar interdependence of objective events among themselves as well as with the subjective (psychic) states of the observer or observers.*

*Permission granted by Princeton University Press. Page xxiv, Carl Jung's foreword to *I Ching*.

### *As Within, So Without*

Whatever happens in your objective or manifest world coincides with impressions made in your subconscious mind. In other words, your objective experiences are a mathematical reflection of your state of consciousness. Your state of consciousness means that which you think, feel, believe, and mentally accept. It means the sum total of your conscious and subconscious impressions and conditioning.

### *The I Ching and Synchronicity*

The hexagram you receive when you ask a question reveals your present state of consciousness and symbolically explains what will follow objectively as a result of the contents of your subconscious mind.

### *His Psychic State and the External Event*

As I write this chapter, the rain is pouring down heavily here in Southern California, and due to the excessive rainfall many areas have been flooded and many homes have been swept away in landslides. During a conversation a young man today told me that a few weeks ago he was in New York City on business, and that one night during his sleep he saw and experienced in a dream his home crumbling before him and being swept away. Also, his wife and son were in danger of drowning and crying for help. Suddenly he awakened, phoned his wife and told her to get out of the house at once. He instructed her to go to a hotel in Los Angeles and notify the authorities. She followed his advice, fleeing with her son, her jewels and a few other immediate possessions. Two hours after she left the house, it collapsed and fell to pieces exactly as her husband had seen it in his dream.

In this instance the objective event (collapse of his house) coincided with his dream, or subjective state. There is no time or space in mind, and since he was in rapport subconsciously with his wife and praying for their mutual guidance and protection, the wisdom of his subconscious revealed to him the immediate danger. Acting on this vision immediately, he was instrumental in saving the lives of his son and wife. This is an example of synchronicity—when the subjective state of his mind paralleled the objective state. Likewise, on consulting the *I Ching*, it reveals events before they have happened objectively. The wisdom of the subconscious knows all and sees all, and when a man trusts it implicitly, he receives its monitions and promptings which bless him in countless ways.

## *Synchronicity of I Ching Saved His Life*

An acquaintance of mine, who occasionally goes to Las Vegas to play roulette, was recently invited by a friend of his to accompany him and a group of men on a chartered plane to Las Vegas. He consulted the *I Ching* and received Hexagram 54, the marrying maiden, which, as he said, indicated misfortune. He declined the invitation and subsequent events verified the accuracy of the *I Ching*; on the return flight of this plane, it was lost in a snowstorm somewhere in the mountains of Nevada. As yet, no trace has been found, even though as many as thirty to forty planes searched the area for days. The hexagram spoke to him symbolically. He was already married; therefore, he transposed its meaning to fit his inquiry, which would be a psychological marriage or union with a group en route to Las Vegas. This would be a mental and emotional agreement on his part constituting a mental marriage. He inferred from the judgment of the Hexagram 54 that it would be an unfortunate experience, and he acted accordingly.

## *How to Develop Your Intuitions*

You must sincerely believe and not just pretend to believe that Infinite Intelligence is guiding and directing you in all ways and in all your thoughts, words and deeds; then you will be led along the right road. Artists, poets, writers and inventors listen to the voice of intuition. Students of the *I Ching* learn to listen to the still small voice. The word "intuition" means "taught from within." It also means "inner hearing." The oldest word for "revelation" meant "that which is heard." This means the Supreme Intelligence within you responds as a feeling, an awareness, an overpowering hunch, intimations and monitions to which you listen and obey. Sometimes intuition comes as a sudden flash or idea to your mind; oftentimes you "hear the voice." Many times it is a voice whose texture, color and substance you can hear as plainly as the voice over the radio.

### *He Heard the Mystic Number 44*

A young man who just returned from a tour of Europe and who has a good knowledge of the *I Ching*, told me how he fell madly in love with a girl in France. He said that she was captivating, charming, fascinating and seductive in her speech, mannerisms, gestures, and to use his own words, "I fell head over heels in love with her." She was pressing him to marry her at once. He said that one night in the hotel in Paris while asleep, he saw a man point to the Number 44 in the *I Ching* and the voice said, "Read and heed." He awakened startled and opened the *I Ching*, which he carries with him always. He said that in perusing it, its instructions were not to go ahead with his proposed marriage. He broke off the engagement, and the next day as he was about to check out of his hotel, two French detectives approached him seeking to know the whereabouts of his former fiancée. They informed him that police in three countries were looking for her for various crimes. She had already been married to four men in different countries without divorcing any of them.

The subconscious of this young man answered him by means of a hexagram which it knew he would obey. This was intuition in the form of the Number 44 hexagram. The subconscious seeks to protect you, and it knew the ulterior motives of the woman in question. The Bible delineates the workings of your subconscious this way: *For as the heavens are higher than the earth, so are my ways higher than your ways, and my thoughts than your thoughts* (Isaiah 55:9). Truly the ways in which your subconscious answers your requests are past finding out.

### *Why Do Predictions by the Kahuna and Psychics Come to Pass?*

This is a question I am frequently asked. Recently a woman said to me that a Kahuna (Hawaiian priest) read her mind perfectly and predicted many things. Then she added, "Immediately following my return from the Island, I called on an old Irish card-reader in Los Angeles, and she read the cards and prognosticated almost exactly the same as the Kahuna, all of which came to pass exactly as foretold by both of them."

### *The Answer to the Question and How It Is Done*

Follow the answer to the question carefully and it will be seen that it is easy to understand and not at all mysterious and strange. It is possible for an intuitive, psychic person in a passive or receptive state of mind, a sort of semi-trance where the conscious mind is partially suspended or slightly in abeyance, to tap the contents of your subconscious mind and reveal the same to your conscious mind. In other words, in a passive state, a sensitive or highly intuitive person tunes in with the fears, impressions, desirable states, subjective acceptance of marriage, divorce, travel, lawsuits, and various other impregnations, be they what they may. The psychic who is tuning in with your subjective feelings and decisions translates these moods and beliefs in his or her own language and foretells accordingly.

### *Your Storehouse and Memory*

Your subconscious is a storehouse of memory, and many suggestions and beliefs have been accepted by you of which your conscious mind is wholly unaware. Your subconscious assumptions, convictions and beliefs become objectified in your world sooner or later unless changed by scientific prayer.

### *The Future Is in Your Mind Now*

You are what you think all day long. Your thought and its manifestation are one in your mind. For example, if you are contemplating divorce, this has already taken place in your mind and can be seen and interpreted by a good medium or psychic, and so can the contents of your subconscious mind—probably not 100%, but let us say at least 90% or more by an outstanding psychic or intuitive person. The plans, decisions, trips and contracts which are now in your mind have not taken place in the three-dimensional plane as yet; time moves slowly from the fourth to the third-dimensional plane, but as you now see, they have already taken place in your mind, which transcends time and space. In your mind the thought and the thing are one. Your desires, ideas and thoughts have form, shape and substance in another dimension of mind and are as real as your hand and can be seen.

### *I Ching and Its Predictions*

When you use the *I Ching*, you are activating your subconscious mind. By being receptive and passive and sincere in your mind, you are actually getting an answer from your deeper mind. It's a sort of mechanical medium for extracting answers which are given to you in figurative and symbolic language, somewhat similar to your own Bible.

### *Predictions for a Group, a Nation or the World*

The *I Ching* will give you answers based on the nature of your question as it deals with the universal subjective mind from which all things flow and from which all things come, to which all things are known, and which permeates all space. Your subconscious is one with this universal mind which is omnipresent. It is therefore possible to predict for a race, nation or group, as well as an individual. Why? Because the majority of human beings do not change very much. They live with the same old beliefs, same old traditions and race concepts, and the same old hates, prejudices and fears. They follow more or less a set pattern which can be easily read by one tuning in psychically or intuitively with the collective unconscious of the masses.

Nostradamus tapped the collective unconscious in the sixteenth century and made the most amazing prognostications in the form of quatrains, many of which came to pass with astounding accuracy. He named such men as Hitler, for whom he used an anagram Hister and accurately described Mussolini together with many others; he predicted the great fire of London and also the bombing of that city in World War II. Yet this was centuries before these occurrences were to take place. The future is truly in our minds now, but it can be changed. There is no inexorable fate. Nothing is foreordained or predestined. As the *I Ching* points out, we can change our future by tuning in with God and getting in harmony with the Cosmic of the universe, and then a future of happiness, health, peace and the life more abundant is assured.

### *The I Ching and Negative Predictions*

When you ask the *I Ching* to comment on your present plans, decisions and the outcome of certain desires you have, it reveals your present state of mind to you. For example, suppose it predicts misfortune? This may mean your motivation is wrong or that you are governed by some irrational emotion or impulse; naturally, the result would not be beneficial. Think good, good follows; think evil, evil follows. *I Ching* tells you if you have deviated from the laws of harmony and the Golden Rule, which is a Cosmic Law, and tells you to get back on the beam and forgive yourself as well as others; re-align yourself with the Infinite Being within you and let the Infinite Ocean of Life, Love, Truth and Beauty flow through you. Then you turn misfortune into good fortune, and the result will be harmonious and victorious for you. Remember the Higher Self of you is Tao, or God, Which always seeks to protect you.

### *How to Counteract Negative Predictions*

The prophecies of Nostradamus in the sixteenth century or those of our modern-day astrologers, psychics, mediums, seers and sensitives throughout the world would mean nothing and could be defied and proved untrue if men knew how to pray. They could thereby change their subconscious, and consequently, their destiny. Prayer eliminates fear, doubt, hate and prejudice from the subconscious of man. That is how he weeds his garden so that only the beautiful flowers may grow. The spiritually minded man, on hearing of something he does not want to come to pass, changes the beginning, and having changed the beginning, he changes the end. This is done by the law of substitution or prayer.

*Instead of praying something out of existence, he prays the condition he wants into existence.* He becomes a producer. You pray by thinking from the standpoint of eternal verities and principles of life, such as realizing that Infinite Intelligence guides and directs me. Divine Love fills my soul. Divine Harmony governs my mind and body. Divine Law and Order govern my life. Divine Love goes before me, making straight and perfect my way. Thinking, speaking, acting and reacting from the standpoint of the One Presence and Power is true prayer. This pattern of prayer frequently repeated with feeling and understanding obliterates the negative patterns of the subconscious mind, making all roads in your life a highway for your God.

### *How She Reversed the Prediction*

An acquaintance of mine was told by a fortune teller that the death card, the ace of spades, indicated her child would die in a few days. Her child had been very ill for a considerable period and was not responding to medical therapy. This woman went home and began to affirm boldly to the child sleeping in the cot: "You are a child of God. God is Life and that is your life now. God lives, moves and has His being in you, and you live, move and have your being in God. God's Healing Power is flowing through you now, and I give thanks for the miraculous healing which I know and believe is taking place now."

In a subjective mood of prayer, she imagined her child running around playing and enjoying himself, radiating health and happiness. She kept this up for five or ten minutes several times a day, feeling and contemplating the reality of it all. On the second day following this prayer process, the child had a remarkable recovery, and she experienced the joy of the answered prayer.

### *Facing the Facts*

The *I Ching*, or *Book of Changes*, is simply stating to you that every condition, circumstance or experience in our lives is simply the outpicturing of assumptions, beliefs and convictions in our subconscious. You must also realize that all sickness, disease, failures, and accidents are but the embodiment of negative ideas or fears in your subconscious mind.

Always remember, scientific prayer can change all negative patterns. . . . *though your sins be as scarlet, they shall be as white as snow; though they be red like crimson, they shall be as wool* (Isaiah 1:18).

## *POINTS TO REMEMBER*

1. Synchronicity means that subjective events and objective events parallel and correlate with each other.
2. Whatever happens in your objective experience has its mental equivalent in your subconscious mind.
3. The hexagram you receive when you ask a question of the *I Ching* reveals your present state of mind and the results that must follow as a result of the contents of your subconscious.
4. Oftentimes your subconscious will reveal what is going to happen in a precognitive dream whereby you see an event before it happens. The reason for this is that your subconscious is all wise and knows what is going to happen before it happens.
5. Students of *I Ching*, and those interested in its Oriental and mystic messages, occasionally receive a hexagram in their sleep, and on looking it up, they receive an answer to their prayer. This is a dramatization of their subconscious mind which intuitively knows to what they will give heed and pay attention. Many lives have been saved by following hexagrams revealed in dreams as well as in the waking state.
6. Intuition means that the wisdom of your subconscious may sometimes speak to you in a voice; inwardly you may have an overwhelming urge to do something, or an idea may come spontaneously as a sort of sudden flash into your conscious, reasoning mind. Intuition means you are taught from within.
7. You may hear the inner voice as one man did recently of the #44 hexagram, and after looking it up he managed to save himself from what would have been a rather tragic experience. The ways of your subconscious are past finding out. This man loves the wisdom of the *I Ching*, and undoubtedly his subconscious knew just how to reveal to him the truth.
8. The future is already in your mind and may be read by highly intuitive or psychic individuals who, in a passive state, tap your subconscious and reveal the future to you.

9. Remember, any thought, idea, plan, decision or purpose you have in your mind also has form, shape and substance and is as real as your hand or watch. This is why they can be seen by a clairvoyant or sensitive, for the beginning and the end are the same in your mind.
10. Whenever you use the *I Ching* in order to get an answer, you are actually activating the wisdom of your subconscious mind, which responds according to the nature of your question.
11. It is possible to predict for a group, a nation or a race because the majority of human beings do not change very much. They live with the same old traditions and beliefs, and they keep repeating the same old patterns endlessly.
12. The *I Ching* tells you if you have deviated from the Law of Harmony and Love and advises you to get back on the beam of God's Glory by aligning yourself with Tao (God). You thereby permit the Life, Love, Truth and Harmony of God to flow through you, bringing good fortune into your life.
13. You can counteract negative predictions by tuning in on the Infinite and thinking from the standpoint of eternal verities and the Principles of Life. A new beginning is a new end, and the negation is wiped out and obliterated from your subconscious mind.
14. There is no inexorable fate, nothing foreordained or predestined. Your thought and feeling control your destiny. A woman who was told by a fortune teller that the cards don't lie and that her child would die, reversed the picture by contemplating that her child's life was God's life and that God was healing him now.
15. Every condition, experience and event in your life is but the outpicturing of patterns of thoughts and beliefs in your subconscious mind.
16. It makes no difference how much you have erred or polluted your deeper mind. The minute you reverse your pattern of thinking and imagining to conform to whatsoever things are true, lovely, noble and God-like, there is an immediate response by your subconscious mind, and the past is forgotten and remembered no more.

# 4

# How the Ageless Wisdom of the I Ching Speaks to You for Guidance

The ageless wisdom of China and India teach that the Living Spirit (God), the Formless, Faceless Being called Tao in China, clothed Itself in matter and descended into materiality. In other words, God imagined Himself to be man and all things in the universe and He became that which He imagined Himself to be. The result of this descent caused man to forget his Divine origin and essence. In Christianity this is termed the fall of man.

The *I Ching* is a constant reminder that buried in each of us, however unevolved, is something that reminds us of our Origin and urges us back to It. Your purpose in life is to liberate, cherish and enlarge that memory, to follow that urge, until the awareness of the Presence of God grows by cultivation into a light and fills you, and you can identify yourself with It.

### *The Opposites in Life*

The foremost scientists in the world have been telling us for a long time that matter and energy are one, and that matter melts into unsubstantial radiation; forever the tangible changes into the intangible. The universe of ours is nothing but waves, a series of densities, frequencies and intensities. I read a newspaper article some time ago where Sir James Jeans indicated that the universe consists of nothing but waves, bottled up waves which we call matter and unbottled waves which we call radiation, or light. In *Genesis* we read the whole story which modern science confirms: *And God said, "Let there be light."*

When the Absolute becomes relative, we experience the opposites. In the Absolute state there is no differentiation. It is a state of oneness, wholeness, completeness and perfection. When It divides Itself into two for the purposes of creation, we experience spirit and matter, large and small, night and day, in and out, male and female, sweet and sour. In other words, you are aware of being alive; you experience contrasts, differences, sensation. As Emerson says, "Every Spirit builds itself a house." You have a body, five senses and the capacity to express your talents, your love, your laughter and your appreciation of things Divine. Emerson explains the opposites beautifully in his essay "Compensation": "Polarity, or action and reaction, we meet in every part of nature; in darkness and light; in heat and cold; in the ebb and flow of waters; in male and female; in the inspiration and expiration of plants and animals; in the centrifugal and centripetal gravity. An inevitable dualism bisects nature, so that each thing is a half, and suggests another thing to make it whole; as spirit, matter; man, woman; odd, even; subjective, objective; in, out; upper, under; motion, rest; yea, nay. Every sweet has its sour; every evil has its good." The *I Ching* points out these opposites, such as good fortune, misfortune; success, failure; etc. It also teaches you how to reconcile these opposites.

### *Reconciling the Opposites*

For example, if a hexagram shows that you have a pattern of failure in your subconscious mind, turn within and harmonize with the Infinite Life-Principle within you, while realizing It cannot fail.

It is Omnipotent. Realize and know you were born to win, to succeed, because the Infinite cannot fail. As you affirm, "Success is mine now through the Power of the Almighty," you will triumph over all obstacles as you persevere in your adherence to the only Presence and Power which never fails. It is Supreme and Omnipotent.

This is how you reconcile the opposites in your mind, such as the thought of success and the thought of failure, which quarrel in your mind. Your thoughts come in pairs. By detaching your attention from the thought of failure and in focusing your devotion and attention instead on success in all your undertakings, then all the power of the Godhead flows to that focal point of attention, and success is assured. Actually, you will be compelled to succeed, for the law of your subconscious is compulsion. Recognize the value of opposition. If you did not have challenge, difficulties or problems, you would never discover your Divinity. The opposites in life enable you to sharpen your mental and spiritual tools, whereby you overcome the obstacle and reconcile the opposites while experiencing the joy of overcoming.

## *Yes and No*

Emerson says, "Every yea has its nay." The Bible says: *Let your communication be, Yea, yea; Nay, nay; for whatsoever is more than these cometh of evil* (Matthew 5:37). The *I Ching* wants you to say "yes" to all ideas which strengthen, heal, bless, inspire, elevate and dignify your life. Say "no" boldly to all teachings, ideas, thoughts, creeds and dogmas which inhibit, restrict and instill fear into your mind. In other words, accept nothing mentally that does not fill your soul with joy.

## *Change and Its Meaning*

An ancient Hebrew meditation lost in antiquity says, "Change perpetual is at the root of all things, and change hath two faces, a face of life, and a face of death." Everything is constantly changing. The formless is forever taking form and the formed is forever returning to the formless. If it is very hot here in California, you can rest assured it is going to cool off. We may now be experiencing a flood in many parts of Southern California which is causing homes to be washed away, but the floods will recede and the sunshine of God's love will reappear. Everything is changing to the opposite. If it is raining somewhere, it also is going to dry up. You can't be sick forever. Everything passes away. St. Theresa said, "Let nothing worry you, let nothing frighten you, let nothing disturb you. Everything passes away but God. God alone is sufficient."

### *The Places Occupied by Lines and Their Significance to You*

The six places in the hexagram are distinguished as follows: The lowest and the topmost are, so to speak, outside the situation. Of these, the lowest is inferior, because it has not yet entered the situation. The uppermost is superior; it is the place of the sage who is no longer involved in worldly affairs, or, under certain circumstances, of an eminent man who is without power. Of the inner places, the second and fourth (from the bottom) are those of officials, or of sons of women. The fourth is the higher, the second inferior to it. The third and fifth (from the bottom) are authoritative places, the former because it is at the top of the lower trigram, and the latter because it is the place of the ruler of the hexagram.*

The places occupied by the lines are differentiated as superior and inferior, according to their relative elevation. As a rule the bottom and the top lines are not taken into account, whereas the four middle lines are active within the time. Of these, the fifth place is that of the ruler, and the fourth that of the minister who is close to the ruler. The third, as the highest place of the lower trigram, holds a sort of transitional position; the second is that of the official in the country, who nevertheless stands in direct connection with the prince in the fifth place. But in some situations the fourth place may represent the wife and the second the son of the man represented by the fifth place. Under certain circumstances the second place may be that of the woman, active within the house, while the fifth place is that of the husband, active in the world without. In short, while any of various designations may be given to a line in a specific place, the varying functions ascribed to the place are always analogous.‡

*Book II, pp. 291–292, *I Ching*, Wilhelm/Baynes, Bollingen Series XIX. Permission granted by the Princeton University Press.

‡*Ibid.* pp. 359–360.

### *The Importance of the Lines*

You will see by the above the importance of the lines in the various hexagrams, and you can intuitively perceive the relationship if you are asking about your employer or your supervisor, who could represent the fifth line. The hexagrams also deal with your family relationship, as the above quotations point out. For example, the salesman could be represented by the second line and his general manager or employer by the fifth line. The nature of your question will determine the significance of the lines and the numbers attached to them. A little practice and a little intuition will aid you immensely. Affirm frequently: "Infinite Intelligence within my subconscious mind guides and directs me and reveals to me the answer, and I intuitively and immediately recognize the answer." Your subconscious mind will respond accordingly.

### *Illustrating the Relationship of Lines to Your Question*

Recently a wife who was separated from her husband asked the *I Ching* if she should go back to him. She received hexagram 42, which indicated to her that it was to her great advantage to return and have a reconciliation. The two trigrams she interpreted as meaning to stir up the spirit of God within her and let love again unite them. The reconciliation and reunion has blessed her beyond her fondest dreams. Conjugal harmony reigns supreme in her home.

### *The I Ching and the Tarot Cards*

I had a conversation a few days ago with a famous international interpreter of the Tarot cards. She told me that she had a very important decision to make, one of the most important in her life. She had asked the Tarot cards first, and then the *I Ching*, and the answers were the same; i.e., to go ahead, good fortune would follow the decision. She asked me, "How do you explain it?" The answer is really very simple. By way of explanation, the Tarot is a pack of picture cards which is the origin of your present-day playing cards.

Each one of the cards pictures the objective, the goal or state of consciousness it designates. Each symbol on the card stands for certain perceptions, faculties, functions—in other words, states of mind. The origin of the cards is lost in antiquity. The ancients stated that certain cards represented love, marriage, divorce, death, journeys, contracts, law, religion, happiness, good fortune, misfortune, etc. Naturally, when you shuffle the cards and think of your question, your subconscious mind selects the cards appropriate to your present state of mind. An intuitive student of the Tarot looks at the cards, which to him or her are an alphabet of your subconscious, and interprets accordingly.

The following analogy might help to clarify the point. Let us suppose you received a letter in Chinese from a friend and you could not read the language. Undoubtedly, you would show it to a Chinese scholar, who would interpret it for you. Cards have no power; they are only pieces of paper, but the ancients who devised these cards attributed a certain meaning and significance to each card, which beliefs are deposited in the mass mind. A good psychic can tap your subconscious and interpret the meaning of the cards, since she is familiar with the esoteric meaning attached to them by the ancient seers.

I explained to this woman that, likewise, in using the *I Ching*, the ancient mystics gave certain meanings to the hexagrams, the lines and the numbers. These meanings are engraved in the collective unconscious of the human race, and when you toss the coins or use yarrow sticks, you are simply activating the age-old wisdom of the universal subconscious, which indwells all men.

## *Lifesaving Premonition*

A few months ago, I suggested to a man that he get a physical checkup from his doctor, as he was constantly complaining of vague pains in his abdominal area. His wife also urged him to do this, but to no avail. He kept taking codeine tablets (a derivative of opium) for the pain, which, of course, alleviated the distress but did not eradicate the cause. One night his wife had a very vivid dream, wherein she saw him being carried to the hospital and operated on for a ruptured appendix. She heard the doctor saying to him, "You have peritonitis. It's very serious."

This woman consulted the *I Ching* for her husband and asked,

"Should not my husband see his doctor at once?" She got hexagram 46 (no moving lines), where it said he should see the great man, which meant to her that he should see his doctor. It was obvious to her what the words "great man" meant. She told her husband about her dream and how the *I Ching* answered her question. He was impressed and agreed to go to the doctor. After an examination, the doctor put him in the hospital at once and told him he had come in the nick of time, as at any moment he could have had a ruptured appendix and peritonitis.

His wife had been praying for guidance for her husband, and her subconscious revealed the true nature of his bodily condition. The *I Ching* confirmed her question—that he should see the great man, which could be a wise spiritual counselor, lawyer, doctor or clergyman depending on what the questioner needed to know. This woman undoubtedly saved her husband's life by her quick action and consultation of the *I Ching*.

### *I Ching Reveals the Secret Powers of your Subconscious*

Professor J. B. Rhine of Duke University has published many books and has gathered an enormous amount of material, well-authenticated and documented, on the extraordinary powers of your subconscious mind. One is clairvoyance, which is the awareness, without use of your five senses, of what is going on elsewhere in the world, enabling you to see it clearly. He has also elaborated at length on precognition (seeing future events before they happen), telepathy (transference of thought from one mind to another), telekinesis (the action of your mind on external objects or matter without physical contact), and retrocognition (your ability to see the past).

The men who invented the *I Ching* and the 64 hexagrams possessed all these gifts of the subconscious and were able to utilize them to understand the laws of the universe and the laws written in the heart of man. They devised a method of divided and undivided lines plus a series of numbers; and through the interaction of these following the tossing of coins by the individual, his subconscious reveals in a symbolic manner the present state of his mind and what his next move should be.

At times I am seized with a deep reverence and a sense of mystic awe when I use the book. It seems and feels as if a human being were talking to me. It is the accumulated wisdom of over 5,000 years speaking to all of us.

## *POINTS TO REMEMBER*

1. The ageless wisdom of China teaches that God, the Formless, Faceless, Life-Principle, clothed Itself in matter and assumed the form of man and all things in the universe. In other words, God imagined Himself to be man, and God became that which He imagined Himself to be. This is called in Christianity "the fall of man," i.e., man meaning mind, which is formless, assumed a form.
2. You are conscious of opposites in life; therefore, you feel yourself to be alive. You are conscious of night and day, ebb and flow, hot and cold, big and little, etc. You have the sense of contrasts, of differences, the sensation of aliveness. Spirit, in order to manifest, must have a body. The opposites in the world are halves of the one whole. The absolute state is one of unalloyed harmony and absolute bliss.
3. Your thoughts come in pairs. Think of riches and the opposite, poverty, comes into your mind. Reconcile the opposites by taking attention away from the thoughts of poverty and giving your attention to God's opulence. As you nourish the idea of wealth, lack and limitation will die and you will begin to express God's riches along all lines.
4. Say "yes" to all the good things in life and "no" to all negation. What you say "no" to in life cannot enter into your experience. "Chant the beauty of the good and stop barking against the bad" (Emerson).
5. Everything is constantly changing. You are changing all the time. You are not the same person you were perhaps a year ago. You have new ideas, new perceptions and insights, and you no longer think, speak and act the same way. The old hymn says, "Change and decay all around I see. Oh, Thou, Who changeth not abide with me." The tangible changes into the intangible and the intangible changes into the tangible.

6. The position of the lines in your hexagram is important. The fifth line is usually the ruler of the hexagram. The bottom line is sometimes referred to in Chinese wisdom as cause and the top line as effect. The nature of your request will reveal the lines which are important to you.
7. There is a subconscious relationship of the *I Ching* to the ancient symbols of the Tarot cards. Many of the symbols depicted in the Tarot correlate with the meaning of many of the hexagrams. Both are products of the subconscious mind of ancient mystics, who devised in picture form and in numerical symbols the great truths of God and the cosmos.
8. A woman consulting the *I Ching* for her husband found it imperative and mandatory that he see the great man (his doctor), which he did, and thereby undoubtedly saved his life.
9. Telekinesis, telepathy, clairvoyance, precognition and retrocognition are all resident in your subconscious mind. The men who wrote the *I Ching* were cognizant of all these powers, utilizing them and devising a system of 64 hexagrams which will answer any question propounded in ancient idiomatic, figurative and allegorical language. This writer has simplified this knowledge and put it in everyday language to aid you in reading your hexagram.

# 5

# A Guide to Terms Used Frequently in the I Ching

The word *judgment* means the verdict of your subconscious mind revealed by your present mental attitude and what you may expect. In other words, it is the conclusion or decision arrived at by the hexagram.

The *image* refers to the inner or esoteric meaning of the lines and how you are to utilize the information in your personal, social or business life.

The words *good fortune* and *misfortune* in the *I Ching* refer to good results from using your subconscious mind in the right way, and misfortune or loss results if you use it negatively. Think good and good follows; think negatively and negation follows.

*No error or no blame* means you are absolved from blame as you have no control over the situation in question. For example, you are not to blame if your plane is delayed by fog or storm.

*Humiliation.* If you are unwilling to think right and do right according to universal principles of harmony and love, humiliation follows as you are going contrary to the laws of life.

*Mistake* in the *I Ching* simply means you can correct any error, and there is no blame. If you make a mistake in addition, for example, and correct it, there is no criticism. You correct mistakes in mental attitudes by turning back to God and thinking according to Divine Law. In other words, you get back on the beam, and the error is corrected.

*Remorse.* You overcome remorse or regret of any kind by realizing no matter how much you may have erred or failed, you can begin to use the law of mind in the right manner. This is accomplished by thinking on whatsoever things are true, lovely, noble and God-like, and there is an immediate reaction on the part of your subconscious mind according to the new mental pattern and imagery. This is why the Bible says: . . . *his mercy is everlasting; and his truth endureth to all generations* (Psalms 100:5). The Law of your mind holds no grudge against you, no more so than do the principles of mathematics or chemistry. When you begin to think right, feel right, act right and do right, the past is forgotten and remembered no more. It is wonderful to know this and to practice it.

*Seeing the great man.* You will have to use your own judgment regarding the great man or the superior man. If it is spiritual advice you need, you should consult someone you trust and respect. It may be legal advice or business counsel you need; in any case, you should arrive at your own decision regarding the type of guidance you need. From an ultimate standpoint, of course, God is your great Counsellor, Advisor and Guiding Light. You can call upon the God-Presence for guidance and It will respond. Whatever mundane advice you need will be made available from the right person for you.

*To cross the water.* Symbolically, your mind is water also, as it takes the shape of any vessel into which it is poured. This means you should come to a clear-cut decision regarding your desire or plan. It is to your advantage to incline your mind vigorously and definitely in the direction of a larger and more wonderful experience. You are moving across the waters (unformed and undefined area of your mind) and will come to a conclusion and definite awareness whereby you reach the point of acceptance in your mind. You are leaving where you are in your mind and mentally establishing a new residence. You are psychologically travelling to a higher position or acceptance of your good. If a journey on land or over sea is indicated, it would also be to your advantage to take the opportunity to travel. If you are thinking about a new position or assignment and you focus your attention on it, the Creative Intelligence within you will always illuminate the matter, for your prayer is a mental and spiritual journey to a new land which is the realization of your heart's desire.

*Chance.* This is defined in the dictionary as the absence of any cause or series of causes of events as they actually happen that can be predicted, understood or controlled. Scientists tell us that this is an ordered, mathematical universe governed, sustained and directed by a Supreme Intelligence with immutable laws, and that it is mathematically impossible for all the essential factors of life to exist on this planet by chance or by a fortuitous confluence of forces or atoms.

Man says something happened by chance, which means he did not perceive the law or principle behind it. Suppose you do not choose your thoughts, images, and reactions, and you permit the mass mind and its propaganda of fear, sickness, accident and misfortune of all kinds to do your thinking for you: then the mass mind controls you, and you do not know what fears and impressions are governing you and controlling your mind. All fears are immersed in the mass or race mind, which impinges on all of us. As you fail to do your own thinking from the standpoint of eternal verities, the mass mind impinges on your mind and does all your thinking for you, and inasmuch as you do not know what these thoughts and feelings are, when they reach a point of saturation in your mind, they are precipitated as accidents, sickness, disability and lack of all kinds. This is chance, not choice. . . . *Choose you this day whom ye will serve* . . . (Joshua 24:15).

Man calls it chance, because he does not know the cause, which is his state of consciousness conditioned by the negation of others and occurring because he refused to think for himself. Emerson said, "Nothing happens by chance; everything is pushed from behind." There is a cause behind every event, even though we don't see it or understand it. It was not by chance that the boy hit the school window when playing ball. A scientist could figure out his stance, the angle at which he threw the ball, the force behind it, the velocity and the wind and other factors to show that the action by the boy and the reaction (broken window) corresponded perfectly.

Choose your thoughts. Choose Divine right action, Divine Law and Order, Divine Love and Divine Peace. Affirm these truths of life, live with them, and you will discover "order is Heaven's First Law." Attend to the noblest, the best and the highest in you, and God's wisdom will guide you to ways of pleasantness and paths of peace. The average man can't calculate the energies and forces operating, and he uses the words fate, accident and chance, but as Emerson says, "Fate is simply the actualization of his thoughts and fits him like his skin."

*Coincidence*. This word is frequently on the lips of many people without much understanding of its psychological implications. Coincidence means to come to occupy the same place in space or the same point in time, a striking occurrence of two or more events at one time apparently by chance—a happening at the same time. Two similar things frequently happen at the same time and in different places. Actions and reactions are universal in life. Your thought and its reaction from your subconscious mind is always happening. The outside or external experience agrees with the inside (your mental attitude).

For example, I was walking down Beverly Drive the other day when I encountered a French actress whom I had known in Paris. She had recently arrived in this country and had been reading *The Power of Your Subconscious Mind* in French.* She said, "I have been looking for you and checking the telephone book, but there were so many Joseph Murphys I was not sure which one to call and I did not know your address. But I had an intense desire to consult with you on a problem." This was what she termed a coincidence, but it was a perfect working of the law of the subconscious mind. The intensity of her thought and desire activated the power of her subconscious and the latter arranged the meeting in Divine order. It was as simple as that.

*See *The Power of Your Subconscious Mind*, by Joseph Murphy, Prentice-Hall, Inc., Englewood Cliffs, N.J., 1963.

### *Her Hexagram*

This actress is a profound student of *I Ching* and asked me to interpret it for her. She wanted the *I Ching* to answer this question: Should I go back to my husband? She cast the coins six times, the technique of which is described in detail in another chapter of this book. She received hexagram 11 with no moving lines (to be discussed later). The title of the hexagram is "Peace."

Biblically I explained to her that the hexagram means *Great peace have they which love thy law and nothing shall offend them* (Psalms 119:165), and that a harmonious reunion was indicated because her state of mind was one of forgiveness and at peace. She agreed that this is the way she felt.

These were not the exact words of the hexagram, but when transposed to ordinary, everyday language she understood it perfectly and agreed that this is the way she felt. Following our conversation she phoned her husband in Paris, and he flew over for the happy reconciliation.

## *POINTS TO REMEMBER*

1. Judgment means the conclusion or verdict of the *I Ching*, more or less the same as when a judge hands down a verdict from the bench. Immediately you are aware of the decision and the consequences.
2. The image refers to the subjective or inner meaning of the lines of the hexagram and how you should utilize the information.
3. No error or no blame: There are many things in life over which you have no control; therefore, you are not to blame. A policeman recently rescued a drowning man, and the man cursed him and abused him. The policeman did the right thing, and of course there was no error or blame.
4. Humiliation follows if you misuse the laws of life. Keep in tune with the Infinite and you will never be humiliated. You are a child of God. Exalt God in the midst of you.
5. Mistake: You had an eraser at the end of your pencil when you went to school. The teacher knew you were going to make mistakes. Don't become angry because you err; you have the oppor-

tunity to correct the mistake. This is how you grow and learn in life. Your mistakes are stepping-stones to your triumph and success in life.

6. Remorse: No use crying over spilt milk. Bless the situation and walk on doing the best you can, realizing God's love floods your mind and heart. Remorse means deep and painful regret for wrongdoing. Literally, it means to be bitten again. Remember, you did the best you could and now that you have grown in wisdom and understanding, you will not repeat it. Forgive yourself and bless the other; then all is forgotten and remembered no more.
7. The great man: This could be someone of integrity whom you respect and from whom you seek advice, a man or woman of high moral and spiritual values. This could apply to legal, medical, or any other professional advice. The greatest Counsellor is God within you. Consult the God-Presence and you will be led objectively to the right attorney or right minister or priest, as the case may be.
8. Cross the water: This means crossing the waters of your mind and coming to a decision. Then the formless takes form, and you are always travelling in your mind from a problem to a solution. This may also mean that a journey over land or sea is favorable.
9. There is no chance, accident or coincidence in a world ruled by law and order. So-called chance is the working of unseen power in your life based on the contents of your subconscious mind. As Emerson says, "Every experience fits you like your skin." Choose your destiny by dwelling on God's eternal verities in your mind. As you sow in your mind, so also shall you reap in experience, conditions and events.
10. Coincidence means two things happening at the same place or point of time. Two things are always occurring—your thought and the reaction of your subconscious to your thought. Coincidence is action of your conscious mind and reaction of your subconscious mind. The outside (experience, condition and event) mirrors the inside. "As within, so without."

# 6

# How to Consult the I Ching

The first step you take for a successful consultation is to quiet your mind, *relax and let go.* Think of the Infinite Intelligence within you and focus your attention on the fact that Its nature is to respond to you. You must be free from all ulterior motives and possess a deep reverence for things Divine. Have a receptive, passive attitude, knowing that you are activating the wisdom of your deeper mind which will respond to you through the *I Ching.*

### *Formulating the Question*

Your question should be clear-cut and definite. There should be nothing vague about it; you must specifically avoid the *either/or* type of question. The following questions are some which were asked in our recent class of the *I Ching*:

Should I get a divorce?
Should I marry this man?
Is it to my advantage to accept this position offered me?
Is it advisable for me to take this assignment overseas?
Is it to my best interest to invest in this land offer?
Will the *I Ching* comment on the future of this gold mine?
Is it to my advantage to invest in this silver mine?
What is the hidden subconscious problem of, let us say, John Jones?
What is my future with this organization?
Will my manuscript be accepted by this publishing company?
What is blocking my prosperity?
What is hindering my healing?
Will my invention be accepted by the Army?

### *Receiving Appropriate Answers*

In the *I Ching*, Wilhelm/Baynes Edition, you receive answers mainly in Oriental symbology and, to a great extent, in figurative language. In this book all I have tried to do is to simplify it as much as possible and render an interpretation which I believe to be the language of the man in the street, the average reader. *You will intuitively perceive the response of the* I Ching *to your particular question.*

### *Two Questions in Her Mind Answered*

As I write this, an old friend has just phoned me from San Francisco asking, "How do I ask the *I Ching* whether I should send my daughter to the University at Berkeley or Brigham Young University in Utah?" I suggested he frame his question as follows: "I would like the *I Ching* to comment on the advisability of sending my daughter to the University of California at Berkeley." I further suggested that he study the answer and then frame the same question regarding the other university: "I would like the *I Ching* to comment on the advisability of sending my daughter to Brigham Young University in Utah," and note the answer. He could then compare the two and decide which was the more favorable. This resolved his problem.

His first question resulted in hexagram 6—Conflict (no moving lines), and the answer to the second question was hexagram 11—Peace, indicating good fortune and success. He sent his daughter to Brigham Young University, where she reports she is very happy.

## *Getting Answers by Means of Coins*

As Chinese coins are hard to get, the value ascribed to heads is usually 2 and tails 3. You can use ordinary U.S. cents (pennies). Take three pennies in your hand and shake them well, then throw them up six times. Give the value of 2 to each heads and the value of 3 to each tails. For example, if you have two heads and one tail in the first throw, the line would be a straight one, the value of which would be 7. The first throw would be the bottom line, as you read the hexagram from the bottom up. Let us say you throw the coins the second time and you have three heads. This would be a divided line: — — 6. The third throw might be, for example, two tails and a head. That would total 8, a broken line: — — 8. The fourth throw might be three tails. That would be 9, a straight line as: —— 9. The fifth throw might be two heads and a tail, which would be 7, a straight line: —— 7. And the sixth, let us say, is three heads, which would be 6, a divided line: — — 6. Now, reading from the bottom up, you construct your hexagram:

— — 6<br>
—— 7<br>
—— 9<br>
(Hexagram 17) — — 8<br>
— — 6<br>
—— 7

## *Key for Identifying the Hexagram*

Please look at the chart on page 76; it lists the 64 hexagrams which are discussed in detail in Chapter 8. This chart is taken from the last page of *I Ching*,* Wilhelm/Baynes Edition, Bollingen Series XIX, Princeton University Press. On the left side under "Trigrams"

*Published by permission of Princeton University Press.

look under "Lower" trigram, reading from top to bottom, which gives you the names and the three lines associated with the eight trigrams. Above the word "Lower" under "Trigrams," you will see the word "Upper," and then you read the eight Trigrams from left to right. This Trigram corresponds to the top three lines of your hexagram. Now take a look at the hexagram we arrived at after tossing the three pennies six times.

You read the hexagram from the bottom line up. The lower first three lines represent Chen:

— — 8
— — 6
—— 7

Look at the upper trigram indicator. Under Tui you will see that it corresponds to the upper three lines of the example hexagram we drew. Now, let your eyes move to the right in a straight line from Chen until your eyes rest under *Tui* marked by the numeral 17. This means you have to look up hexagram 17, which means Following. This is the simple procedure of finding your hexagram 17.

— — 6
—— 7
—— 9
— — 8
— — 6
—— 7

*Moving Lines*

In the hexagram we drew you will note there are three moving lines. The lines marked 6 and 9 move to their opposites, generating a new hexagram. The lines marked 8 and 7 remain stationary. The line marked 6 changes into its opposite, a straight line marked —— 7; the fourth line marked 9 changes to its opposite, which is a broken line — — 8. The top line marked 6 changes also to its opposite marked 7, a straight line —— 7. Now you have a new hexagram. Start from the bottom up. —— 7 remains the same. The line 6 is now —— 7. The line — — 8 remains the same. The line —— 9 changes to its opposite, — — 8. The fifth line, —— 7, remains the same. And the top line — — 6 becomes ——— 7. The new hexagram starting from the bottom up reads as follows:

——— 7
——— 7
— — 8
— — 8
——— 7
——— 7

This gives you a new hexagram, 61, which indicates the outcome or the result when you follow the findings of your first hexagram.

### *The Lines which Do Not Move*

The lines which become 7 and 8 never move. Whenever you have lines in a hexagram such as 6 and 9, these are moving lines, and give rise to another hexagram. Therefore, there can't be more than two hexagrams in such cases. The first hexagram could be called the diagnosis and the second the prognosis. I have gone into somewhat exhaustive detail in constructing and explaining the structure of a hexagram, as I wish to present it in the simplest way possible.

### *Importance of Lines 6 and 9*

When lines are marked 6 or 9, you will read and follow what is delineated. It may be that the comments on the lines 6 or 9 may contradict the judgment and the image of the hexagram. When they do, you follow the instructions of the lines rather than the judgment of the hexagram.

### *When There Are No Moving Lines*

When there are no lines 6 and 9 in your hexagram, you pay no attention to the lines of the hexagram. You read the contents of the judgment and the image, which is the answer to your question.

### *Reading the Lines in Your First Hexagram*

The only lines you pay attention to and apply in your life are the lines 6 and 9 in your *first* hexagram. When these change to another hexagram, you do *not* read the lines of the second hexagram, just the judgment, the image. The lines in the second hexagram are always ignored.

### *7 and 8 Numbers*

You will never see any reference to these lines in your hexagram, since they are not taken into consideration in lineal interpretation.

### *A Simple Way to Change a Hexagram When Change Is Indicated*

Suppose your hexagram is as follows:

| | | | |
|---|---|---|---|
| | — — 6 | | ——— 7 |
| | — — 6 | | ——— 7 |
| This is | ——— 7 | This changes | ——— 7 |
| Hexagram 34 | ——— 9 | to Hexagram 12 | — — 8 |
| | ——— 9 | | — — 8 |
| | ——— 9 | | — — 8 |

You would read the judgment and image of hexagram 34 and the meanings given to all the lines marked 9 and 6. When *I Ching* says 9 at the beginning, this means the bottom line with which you started and so on up the hexagram. In reading the second hexagram, which would be the outcome of your request, provided you followed the instructions given to you in the first hexagram, you read the judgment and the image and then ignore all the lines of the second hexagram.

### *When the Hexagram Does Not Change*

When you draw a hexagram with no moving lines (6's and 9's), you follow the interpretation under judgment and image and ignore the data under the lines.

### *Your Motivation Is Important*

The purity of your motives is important when asking questions. I might add that the illumined seers and mystics of *I Ching* who devised this method of extracting wisdom from your subconscious have a built-in mechanism in this numerical system which prevents its use for negative purposes of any kind.

### *Numbers and the I Ching*

When we study the atomic structure and number of all the elements, we find the unbroken order of the number of positive charges or protons in the nucleus of an atom in a given element, and, therefore, also the number of electrons normally surrounding the nucleus. Pythagoras said the world was governed by number and motion, which is true. The only difference between one substance and another is the number and rate of motion of electrons and protons revolving around a nucleus.

The interaction of lines and numbers in the *I Ching* represents powers, attributes and states of mind within you. Symbolically speaking, numbers represent potencies and qualities of the one Power and Presence. The hexagram reveals how you are using that Power, constructively or destructively. There is nothing good or bad, but thinking makes it so. It is your use of this Inner Power that determines whether the result is good or bad for you.

### *When Lines Seem to Contradict the Judgment and Image*

In such instances, preference must be given to what the moving lines (6's and 9's) say. Obviously, there is some hidden and particular reason of which you are not consciously aware, but your subconscious is cognizant of the special reason.

### *When Two Hexagrams Are Received in Response to Your Question*

The two hexagrams may be very dissimilar and contrary in their meaning. In reality there is no opposition between them, as they are simply reminding you of the first phase and later results of the same event. In other words, a particular mine might be very productive in the beginning but dwindle out after a while. Your second hexagram would therefore point to the result or outcome of your question.

### *The Answer Does Not Exceed Two Hexagrams*

Regardless of the number of moving lines in the first hexagram, the response to your question does not exceed two hexagrams.

## *POINTS TO REMEMBER*

1. Adopt a quiet, peaceful, receptive attitude of mind, knowing that Infinite Intelligence within your subconscious knows the answer and gives it to you through the *I Ching*.
2. Your question should be to the point, clear and definite. Questions should never be vague or nebulous.
3. You may ask any legitimate question. Do not treat the matter lightly. Ask the question with a certain reverence for the wisdom of the ages.
4. The answers given you in this book under each hexagram are free from Oriental symbolism and idiomatic and figurative language. You will find short, concise answers couched in the language of everyday life.
5. If you are wondering which college or university to choose for the further education of your son or daughter, formulate a question separately for each university and select the one with the appropriate answer.
6. The quickest way to get answers is through tossing coins. Use ordinary U.S. coins, such as pennies. Toss three coins six times, which must be the same size and same kind. Heads are given the value of 2 and tails 3. After six throws of three coins (U.S. cents), your hexagram is formed. (Some give the value of two to tails and three to heads. It really makes no difference, as the only thing important is the value you give to them. In this book, follow the value of two for heads and three for tails.)
7. There is no difficulty in identifying the hexagram. Consult the chart appearing immediately before Hexagram 1. The three lower lines of your hexagram will reveal the trigram in the left-hand vertical corner, and the three upper lines of your hexagram can be found by looking directly opposite the upper trigram from left to right. Then let your eyes move in a straight

line to the right of your lower trigram until you are directly under the upper trigram, and you will find the number of the hexagram in a square.

8. Moving lines in your first hexagram are 6's and 9's. Six changes to 7, and 9 changes to 8, bringing about a new hexagram.
9. Lines 7 and 8 are stationary and do not move. They are a part of the structure of the hexagram.
10. Read the interpretations under lines marked 6 and 9, such as 6 in the second lines says . . . , or 9 in the fifth line says . . . , etc. If a line or lines seem to contradict the comment or judgment and image, follow the instruction of the lines rather than the text of the above.
11. When there are no moving lines in your hexagram, you pay no attention to the lines of the hexagram. You read the material in the judgment and image and follow that.
12. You do not take any lines into consideration in the second hexagram, just the judgment and image only.
13. Your motivation is important. Let the Golden Rule and the Law of Love govern you when you use the *I Ching*.
14. You cannot use the *I Ching* for any negative or ulterior purposes, as the ancient seers have a built-in mathematical system contained in the interaction of lines and numbers. To state it simply, your subconscious is a recording machine, and it records your silent motives and the nuances of your thought, so you can't fool it. If you go into your subconscious with negation, you will reap nothing but negation magnified and multiplied in your life.
15. When two hexagrams are received in response to your query, the first hexagram represents the incipient stage and the second hexagram the outcome or ultimate result.
16. The answer does not exceed two hexagrams.

# 7

# How to Interpret the Mystic Hexagrams of the I Ching

### *Yang and Yin Lines*

Yang and Yin represent the male (Yang) and female (Yin) principles. In simple, everyday language, insofar as you are concerned, look upon them as your conscious and subconscious, or your thought and feeling. Yang lines are undivided. Yin lines are divided. Yang lines are denoted by 7 and 9; i.e., they are straight lines. Yin lines are denoted by 6 and 8; i.e., they are divided lines. The straight line 9 in a hexagram changes into its opposite, a divided line, — — 8; and the line 6, which is a divided line, changes into its opposite, which is 7, or a straight line.

### *Your Interpretation*

Think quietly about the hexagram you receive, realizing at the same time that the wisdom of your deeper mind will rise up and come clearly into your conscious mind, thereby enabling you to recognize and intuitively know the answer.

## *I Ching Is Fourth Dimensional*

The fourth dimension of life is all around us and interpenetrates this plane. You go there every night when you sleep. It is another dimension of mind. Oftentimes you receive answers to life's problems as you dream; many times you see events before they happen; sometimes it is weeks or months before the events dreamed about occur in this three-dimensional or objective plane of life. The experiences, events, successes and disappointments, if any, that are going to happen to you are already subsistent in your deeper mind. Your present state of mind determines your future; therefore, your future is your present thinking and beliefs made manifest. The beginning and the end are the same in your fourth-dimensional mind. In other words, the thought and the thing are one, as there is no time or space in the next dimension of your mind.

For example, I said to a friend of mine the other day, "You are planning to go to Hawaii, aren't you?" He said, "Yes. How did you know? No one knows anything whatever about my proposed trip." I explained to him that his thought of Hawaii and the trip were one in his mind and that mentally he had already travelled there. I added that his thoughts, plans, and ideas have form, shape and substance in the next dimension of mind and that they can be perceived clairvoyantly by many and intuitively by others. The ideas and plans you have in your mind now are as real as your hand or head. The idea of anything is the reality of it.

Suppose all the airplanes in the world were destroyed by some holocaust; an engineer who had the idea of a motor in his mind could reconstruct one in his workshop, and the factories of the world could create them by the million. The real car is in the mind of the engineer.

## *I Ching Sees Fourth-Dimensionally*

Suppose you were planning to go by automobile from Los Angeles to St. Louis, Missouri, and in the meantime you had been reading about the flooding of the rivers and roads here, there and everywhere in the West and South. Objectively and according to your five senses, you would not know the conditions of the road from Los Angeles to St. Louis, but a navigator on an airplane having flown low over the route, with the help of his telescopic and photographic apparatus, could perceive clearly the condition of the roads, washed out bridges, big boulders on the main highways and other impassable conditions. He would see the conditions from a higher level and be able to communicate what he perceived to you. You would thereby be protected and saved from possible tragedy due to his capacity to see at higher levels. This is an analogy of fourth-dimensional seeing.

### *I Ching and Prescience*

Having read this far, you are fully cognizant of the fact that you call upon the higher aspects of your mind when you use either the coin method or the yarrow stalk procedure. Your deeper mind is prescient; i.e., it has knowledge of things before they are objectively experienced or happen in the outer world. It has foreknowledge of that which is to come, and the *I Ching* reveals to you your present state of mind, also that which is to happen based on subconscious conditioning and acceptances.

### *Fourth-Dimensional Seeing*

If you were an aviator flying some distance above a railroad track you would be able to observe two trains approaching each other on the same track. The engineers on each train are not aware of the impending crash, yet the aviator flying overhead sees the danger immediately and can warn them in time, thereby preventing a crash and resultant tragedy. Likewise, you can use the *I Ching* for similar purposes. The hexagram you receive may warn you that your proposed action may result in loss; therefore, you have the opportunity to get back on the beam and correct your mental attitude and modify your approach to the particular venture in question.

### *Asking a Question for Another Person*

If someone asks you to consult the *I Ching* regarding some matter of importance, both of you should agree on the nature of the specific request. The person may be physically located a distance from you, or the query could be the result of a telephone call from the other person. Follow this procedure: Think of the person quietly and then throw the coins six times as previously outlined, focussing your attention on the question. Detach yourself as much as possible from your surroundings and get completely absorbed in one thing—the answer and the response you receive will reveal to you what you seek to know. Always rely on that intuitive faculty within you which enables you to see clearly the inner meaning of the hexagram.

### *The Yarrow Stalk Technique Compared with the Coin Technique*

This is a time-consuming procedure and has no real advantage over the coin tossing technique. The whole procedure depends on your attitude of mind. The complex yarrow stalk procedure outlined in books on the *I Ching* is not at all necessary. It is obvious to all who understand to any degree the working of the subconscious mind that the ritual prescribed favors suggestion by making a powerful appeal to the imagination, thereby activating the spiritual process of the subconscious. You will get the same results by adapting a passive, psychic and receptive state of mind before using the coins.

### *Recognizing the Response*

A medical doctor, who has been a student of the *I Ching* for twenty years or more, made this request: "I would like the *I Ching* to comment on my health." The *I Ching* advised him to see the "great man," which could mean a man of the highest spiritual calibre or a man of great wisdom, such as an outstanding doctor, lawyer or other specialist whom he respected and honored. In this case the doctor deduced from the hexagram that he should see one of his colleagues, which he did. An X-ray examination revealed a lesion of which he was not conscious. He had it attended to at once, and since then his health has improved in a wonderful way.

This physician realized that his subconscious intuitively grasped the presence of the lesion and that it revealed its conclusion in the advice given in the hexagram. By his prompt action he felt that he undoubtedly averted much more trouble later on.

Remember, there is always a solution to every problem, an answer to every question, a way out when lost in the woods. The reason for this is that only the Infinite Intelligence within you knows the answer.

## *Right and Wrong*

A man said to me the other day that he had great difficulty in determining whether the God-Self in him was talking to him or whether his negative emotions were prompting him. He had been reading articles in the paper where some sectarian devotees of a particular mountain retreat claimed that God told them to kill other members of the group. Similarly, some time ago there was an article in the paper wherein a man said God told him to kill his mother-in-law.

These impulses to kill or destroy cannot be of God—the Author only of perfect good. These come from the negative, destructive thinking of the person, and his thoughts generate emotions which get snarled up in his subconscious mind; therefore, it is his own subconcious playing back the recording he engraved on it. Murder is of the heart, and a man having murderous, hateful thoughts actually hears his own voice, "Kill her." What he takes into his subconscious he draws out.

## *How to Be Certain of True Guidance*

First of all, your motivation must be right based on the Golden Rule and the Law of Love, which means goodwill to all men. If a man's motives are ulterior, if he is full of fear and resentment, his subconscious will play back to him exactly what he has recorded, and the impulses and promptings which come to him will, of course, be of a negative nature.

Adopt this procedure and affirm meaningfully: "My motivation is right. I radiate love and good will to all men and women, and I sincerely wish for them all the blessings of life. I believe implicitly in a God of Love, and I know the promptings, whisperings and impulses which come from the Infinite Intelligence within me are always lifeward and Godward. Everything I aspire to in life and every question I ask comes to me only one way—that is, in Divine law and order—and I recognize the *lead* which comes clearly into my conscious, reasoning mind." Convey this prayer by repetition and sincerity to your subconscious mind, and you will have no trouble recognizing true Divine guidance. *For God is not the author of confusion, but of peace . . .* (I Corinthians 14:33).

### *The I Ching and True Guidance*

Oftentimes you will find the *I Ching* will instruct you to desist from a certain course; the reason for this is obvious. It may be that you are under the sway of negative emotion, and the course you are taking would lead to loss and limitation. You can always get back "on the beam" and insist on Divine law and order in all departments of your life. There must be no tendency in you towards deceit, trickery or taking advantage of others, as this negative attitude would only bring misery, pain and loss of all kinds into your experience.

Follow the injunction: . . . *whatever ye would that men should do to you, do ye even so to them . . .* (Matthew 7:12).

## *POINTS TO REMEMBER*

1. Yang and Yin lines in Chinese symbology refer to the male and female principle within all of us. Yang lines are straight lines such as 9 and 7. Yin lines are divided, such as 8 and 6.
2. Think quietly about the hexagram you receive, realizing at the same time that the wisdom of your subconscious is speaking through the *I Ching*, giving you the appropriate answer.
3. *I Ching* deals with the fourth-dimensional phase of life; i.e., the mind which transcends your ego or intellect. Desires, ideas, thoughts and plans you have possess form, shape and substance in the next dimension of life and may be seen and intuitively perceived by a highly psychic or intuitive person.
4. *I Ching* sees fourth-dimensionally, and when you ask a question, there takes place an interaction between the lines and the numbers dramatizing the present state of your mind and the future. Your future is always your present state of mind made manifest.
5. You are calling on the higher aspects of your mind whether

you use the coin method or yarrow stalks. Your deeper mind possesses foreknowledge of that which is to come. If it is of a negative nature, you can change it by tuning in on the Infinite and becoming a focal point for the harmony, peace and joy of God to govern, guide and direct you.

6. You may ask a question for another. Both of you should agree on the specific question. Focus your attention on the question, knowing the right answer will come to you, and it will be done unto you as you believe.
7. There is no particular advantage in using the yarrow stalk procedure. The whole point is a receptive attitude of mind and a recognition and reverence for the wisdom of the ages. There is no particular virtue in yarrow stalks or in coins. Both are made of the same primordial substance, and the only difference is due to the number and rate of motion of the electrons and protons revolving around a nucleus. There is nothing good or bad, pure or impure, clean or unclean, but thinking makes it so.
8. You will intuitively recognize the response you receive by realizing Infinite Intelligence is revealing the answer to you through the *I Ching*, which is simply a mathematical medium you have chosen to use. The principle of mathematics existed before any man walked the earth and before any church was formed on the face of the earth. The Eternal Principles underlying this mathematical and ordered universe always existed and are the same yesterday, today and forever.
9. Your subconscious is like a recording machine; it plays back to you what you have impressed upon it. When you are full of love and goodwill to all and your mind is free from trickery, deceit and chicanery of any kind, and when your motivation is pure, noble and God-like, and when you aspire that all things in life come to you in Divine law and order, then the impulses, promptings, monitions and ideas which well up within you will be onward, upward, lifeward and Godward.
10. When you ask for Divine guidance, realize Infinite Intelligence is all-wise, knows all and sees all. Its tendency is always lifeward—the abundant life. Trust the Guiding Principle, while knowing It responds to you as you call upon It. Your motivation must be wholesome and based on the Golden Rule of Life, i.e.,

you wish for all men what you wish for yourself. The *lead* will come to you. You will always recognize it. *Remember, God is not the author of confusion, but of peace* . . . (I Corinthians 14:33).

11. Sometimes the hexagram you receive may inform you to desist from a certain course, as you may be under the sway of a negative emotion. Studying the hexagram, you can get back on the beam of God's glory by filling your mind with the truths of God, which crowd out of your mind everything unlike God.

| TRIGRAMS<br>UPPER ▶<br>LOWER ▼ | Ch'ien ☰ | Chên ☳ | K'an ☵ | Kên ☶ | K'un ☷ | Sun ☴ | Li ☲ | Tui ☱ |
|---|---|---|---|---|---|---|---|---|
| Ch'ien ☰ | 1 | 34 | 5 | 26 | 11 | 9 | 14 | 43 |
| Chên ☳ | 25 | 51 | 3 | 27 | 24 | 42 | 21 | 17 |
| K'an ☵ | 6 | 40 | 29 | 4 | 7 | 59 | 64 | 47 |
| Kên ☶ | 33 | 62 | 39 | 52 | 15 | 53 | 56 | 31 |
| K'un ☷ | 12 | 16 | 8 | 23 | 2 | 20 | 35 | 45 |
| Sun ☴ | 44 | 32 | 48 | 18 | 46 | 57 | 50 | 28 |
| Li ☲ | 13 | 55 | 63 | 22 | 36 | 37 | 30 | 49 |
| Tui ☱ | 10 | 54 | 60 | 41 | 19 | 61 | 38 | 58 |

Key for Identifying the Hexagrams

Permission to use the 64 Hexagrams in sequence and the Trigram meanings thereof granted by Princeton University Press.

# 8

# Your I Ching Hexagrams and Their Meanings

Consult the chart (or key) on the preceding page when you wish to find the hexagram that you have created. Instructions are given on page 61, Chapter 6, for constructing your hexagram in seeking advice. There are sixty-four hexagrams possible as can be seen from the key. Each hexagram grouping will now be discussed in detail. The key numbers for the structure of a hexagram (see key) are the identifying numbers for the hexagrams in the analyses which follow.

## 1. Ch'ien/The Creative

**above Ch'ien, The Creative, Heaven**

**below Ch'ien, The Creative, Heaven**

The ancient Chinese mystics explained that in order to create the universe and man, God divided Himself into two parts, male and female, and from the interaction of these two, called Yang (male) and Yin (female), was born the whole universe. Spirit chooses or decides whether there shall be a universe. Mystery schools refer to this Spirit as the Grand Architect of the universe. It chooses and selects and It also initiates the creative process by releasing the images of what It wants to the female aspect of Itself, which accepts the thought patterns and brings it forth. Many symbols are used in the various religions of the world when referring to the Creative Power. Oftentimes It is called the Father, Mother, God, Yang and Yin, Active and Passive Principle, and Adam and Eve.

For all practical purposes, look upon Ch'ien first as the male principle in you, i.e., your conscious mind which has the capacity to select and choose and thus has the power of initiative. You can select the images, the thought patterns you give to your subconscious mind, which is the fabricator, and it will reproduce faithfully whatever you impress upon it. Your conscious mind, therefore, can be compared to Spirit, because you create your conditions, experiences and events by the same process by which God created the sun, moon, stars and the galaxies in space and all things therein contained. You are made in the image and likeness of God. Your mind is God's mind and your spirit is God's Spirit. Your conscious, reasoning, selective, volitional mind is not absolutely pure, whole, immaculate and perfect like Spirit but it corresponds to Spirit in its functional capacity, i.e., its power to select and to initiate. The purpose of this explanation is to simplify matters for you and to cause you to see that these hexagrams bear an intimate relationship with your state of mind and your own particular world.

*The Judgment*

The illumined conscious mind chooses only God's ideas and eternal verities; and, feeling the reality of these truths, they sink into the subconscious mind and, like seeds, they come forth after their kind.

*The Image*

God is The Living Spirit Almighty, The Only Presence, Cause, Power and Substance. As you join up mentally with this Supreme Power, It becomes active and potent in your life.

*The Lines*

Nine at the bottom place: *In quietness and in confidence lie your strength. . . .* (Isaiah 30:15). Be still and quiet for the time being, the right way will unfold in due season.

Nine in the second place: It is to your advantage to seek counsel from someone whom you respect and trust. Know that God guides you to the right man for you.

Nine in the third place: When you come home from work, relax, let go, detach yourself from all the vexations and strife of the day and contemplate the Presence of God within you. Know that the harmonizing power of God is flowing through you. Know and claim: *. . . there is no power but of God* (Love) . . . (Romans 13:1). Walk in love and all will be well.

Nine in the fourth place: Come to a clear-cut decision, while knowing and believing that Divine right action is governing you, and *Let all your things be done with charity* (I Corinthians 16:14).

Nine in the fifth place: It would be a good idea to visit a spiritually minded man for advice and counsel. Know that you are Divinely guided in all your ways. Good fortune is yours.

Nine at the top: . . . *Thou shalt love thy neighbor as thyself* (Leviticus 19:18). . . . *he that dwelleth in love dwelleth in God* . . . (I John 4:16). Salute the Divinity in all those around you. Be kind and considerate and wish for all of them health, happiness, peace and all the blessings of life. Forgive yourself for harboring any negative thoughts about yourself or others. . . . *walk in love* . . . (Ephesians 5:2).

## 2. K'un/The Receptive

— —
— — **above K'un, The Receptive, Earth**
— —
— —
— — **below K'un, The Receptive, Earth**
— —

This is the female aspect of God, sometimes referred to as the Virgin Mary, Sophia of the Persians, the Passive Principle, the Holy Ghost, the Universal Subconscious, the Great Fabricator, or the Law. It is called the Heart (subconscious) in the Bible; also, the Law, the woman, and the wife. The Bible says the husband shall be head of the wife, meaning that whatever the male aspect impregnates the female aspect of itself with, the latter brings it forth in the image and likeness of the pattern or image implanted in it.

For our purposes in this book, look upon this second hexagram K'un as your own subconscious mind, which is your creative medium. Your subconscious has the "know-how" of all creation. Your conscious, choosing mind selects an idea, plan or purpose, and when you turn over this idea with faith and confidence to your deeper mind, it brings it to pass in its own way. The Universal Subconscious, of which your subconscious is an integral part, knows how the whole world came into being. Your subconscious created your body and knows all the processes and functions of it. It is one with boundless wisdom and Infinite Intelligence. Remember, your subconscious mind will bring forth to fruition any pattern your conscious mind focuses attention on and nourishes and sustains quietly and with confidence. Your subconscious* is that phase of your mind which brings all things to pass.

*The Judgment*

Your subconscious is pregnant with all the powers, attributes and qualities of God. It is called Mary in our Bible, who is already pregnant with the Holy Ghost, meaning the Holy Spirit or the Spirit of Wholeness. It is pregnant with all the powers of the God-head and has the know-how of accomplishment. You can use the powers of your subconscious two ways: Think good and good will follow; think evil and evil will follow. Think on whatsoever things are true, noble and God-like and you will reap a wonderful harvest of health, happiness and peace.

*The Image*

You can sow whatever you like in your subconscious in the same manner as you sow seeds in your garden. Let your dominant conviction be "God loves, governs, guides and directs me in all ways," and your outer world will magically melt into the image and likeness of your dominant conviction.

*The Lines*

Six in the bottom place: . . . *be careful to maintain good works* . . . (Titus 3:8). Cleanse your mind of ill will and resentment. You know when you have forgiven others because you can meet them in

*Read *The Power of Your Subconscious Mind* by Dr. Joseph Murphy, Prentice-Hall, Inc., Englewood Cliffs, N.J., 1963.

your mind and there is no longer any sting there, somewhat similar to the hypothetical example that you may have had an abscess a year ago which was very painful. You now have a memory but no sting. To understand all is to forgive all.

Six in the second place: *And whatsoever he doeth shall prosper* (Psalms 1:3). Know that whatever you do will prosper and that Divine right action and success are yours right now.

Six in the third place: Realize God is the source of your supply and that God is your Boss, your Ruler and your Guide. Give all honor and glory to God. Do not boast or brag. Realize this truth: "I can do all things through the God-Power Which strengtheneth me."

Six in the fourth place: *Be careful for nothing, but in every thing by prayer and supplication with thanksgiving let your requests be made known unto God* (Philippians 4:6). Relax, let go. Keep still and quiet. Trust God and all will be well.

Six in the fifth place: *Her ways are ways of pleasantness and all her paths are peace* (Proverbs 3:17). Whatever you do will prosper. *The joy of the Lord is your strength* (Nehemiah 8:10).

Six at the top: Whatever conflict is in your mind, realize that you inevitably overcome evil with good. Do not fight the negative thoughts in your mind. Supplant them with constructive thoughts of love, harmony and peace. Light dispels darkness, as darkness is absence of light. Sense your oneness with God now and God's River of Peace will flow through you bringing peace to the troubled mind.

## 3. CHUN/DIFFICULTY AT THE BEGINNING

— —<br>
——— **above K'an, The Abysmal, Water**<br>
— —<br>
— —<br>
— — **below Chen, The Arousing, Thunder**<br>
———

*The Judgment*

*. . . he that endureth to the end shall be saved* (Matthew 10:22). This means the solution will come through stick-to-itiveness and perseverance, knowing that through the power of the Almighty you can achieve your goal. Think right, feel right, act right and be right.

*The Image*

Grapple with your project courageously, while realizing every problem is Divinely outmatched. Realize that Divine law and order govern all your activities.

*The Lines*

Nine at the bottom place: *Commit thy way unto the Lord; trust also in him; and he shall bring it to pass* (Psalms 37:5). Keep on persevering while realizing that Infinite Intelligence in your subconscious reveals to you everything you need to know and that you are Divinely guided to the right people who cooperate with you.

Six in the second place: *Rest in the Lord* (Law) *and wait patiently for him* (Psalms 37:7). Sit steady in the boat and quiet your mind. Don't let anything bother you. Wait patiently for the time being and there will be a Divine solution and a harmonious ending.

Six in the third place: . . . *their strength is to sit still* (Isaiah 30:7). Be not anxious. Remain where you are and know the dawn appears and all tne shadows will flee away. Sit still, for the present.

Six in the fourth place: *Wait on the Lord; be of good courage, and he shall strengthen thine heart: wait, I say, on the Lord* (Psalms 27:14). This means that you can't force the seed in the soil to grow. You simply water and fertilize it and thereby accelerate its growth. Likewise, the desire of your heart now deposited in your subconscious mind (called the Lord) will come to pass at the right time and in Divine order.

Nine in the fifth place: *But I say unto you, that you resist not evil* . . . (Matthew 5:39). You overcome evil with good. When you resist or fight something in your mind, you magnify it and you set the law of reversed action into operation. In other words, you get the opposite of what you pray for when you fret, fuss, fume and get angry. Quiet and still your mind and contemplate that all things come to pass for you in *Divine law and order*.

Six at the top: *Continue in prayer and watch in the same with thanksgiving* (Colossians 4:2). Be faithful every step of the way and you will experience the joy of accomplishment.

## 4. Meng/Youthful Folly

——
— — above Ken, Keeping Still, Mountain
— —
— —
—— below K'an, The Abysmal, Water
— —

*The Judgment*

*That our sons may be as plants grown up in their youth . . .* (Psalms 144:12). *Remember now thy Creator in the days of thy youth . . .* (Ecclesiastes 12:1). When we are young we are immature. We go to school to learn and to be disciplined, not to tell the teacher how to teach or how to run the school. We must have a hunger and thirst for wisdom and respect for authority and the wisdom of the ages; then we will advance along all lines.

*The Image*

True education consists not only in knowing secular subjects and the sciences, but also the spiritual values of life. We must learn that we are here to glorify God and to enjoy Him forever. We must engage in spiritual athletics and in the discovery of the infinite treasure house within.

*The Lines*

Six at the bottom: *Train up a child in the way he should go and when he is old, he will not depart from it* (Proverbs 22:6). *The rod and reproof give wisdom; but a child left to himself bringeth his mother shame* (Proverbs 29:15). There is no love without discipline and no discipline without love. The above truths are very relevant today.

Nine in the second place: *Judge not, and ye shall not be judged; condemn not, and ye shall not be condemned* (Luke 6:37). There are many difficult people in the world. Adjust to them, and be tolerant. Withhold your judgment. You would not be angry or resentful of a hunchback or a cripple. Many are mentally warped. Bless them and walk on. You are the only thinker in your universe, and *you are responsible* for the way you think. Discipline your thought, feelings, actions and reactions and conform always to the Golden Rule.

Six in the third place: *To every thing there is a season, and a time to every purpose under the heaven . . . a time to plant and a time to pluck up that which is planted* (Ecclesiastes 3:1–2). Wait—this is not the time to plant or embrace. . . . *a time to embrace and a time to refrain from embracing* (Ecclesiastes 3:5).

Six in the fourth place: "Where there is no vision the people perish." Your vision is what you give your attention to, what you are looking at mentally. You must have a foundation under your mental image. You must be practical. Your imagination must be disciplined, controlled and directed wisely and judiciously. Your dream or idea will never see the light of day except it is deposited and felt as true subconsciously.

Six in the fifth place: *Verily I say unto you, Except ye be converted and become as little children, ye shall not enter into the kingdom of heaven* (Matthew 18:3). A child is open and receptive and is full of trust. Similarly, let your mind be open and receptive to the truth that thoughts are things, that what you feel you attract, and that what you imagine you become. Believe in good fortune and you shall experience it. To believe is to accept something as true and to be alive to that truth. You are belief expressed.

Nine at the top: To forgive and to condone are not the same thing. You forgive your young boy for stealing apples but you don't condone it; otherwise, he will probably grow up to be a thief. You discipline him, perhaps by assigning him tasks. Or, he might be trained in this manner: If he gets 50¢ a week pocket money, he does not receive any money for two weeks; then at the end of that time, he takes the dollar which he would ordinarily have earned over to Mrs. Jones for the apples which he borrowed and forgot to pay for. When you discipline a boy or anyone else, the primary objective is to see to it that he conforms to the Golden Rule.

## 5. Hsü/Waiting (Nourishment)

— —
—— **above K'an, The Abysmal, Water**
— —
——
—— **below Ch'ien, The Creative, Heaven**
——

*The Judgment*

It is to your advantage to direct your mind and focus your attention on higher aspects of living or on greater and larger experiences. Move from where you are in your mind to a new decision. You are always travelling in your mind from one place to another location. Accept the inner and outer journey to a greater measure of life and continued expansion along all lines.

*The Image*

. . . *I will rain bread from heaven for you* . . . (Exodus 16:4). Live in the joyous expectation of the best and invariably the best will come to you. Accept the blessings of life to which you are increasingly open and receptive.

*The Lines*

Nine at the bottom: . . . *In quietness and in confidence shall be your strength* . . . (Isaiah 30:15). Attend to all routine matters, knowing that all things are working together for your good. The way opens up in Divine order through Divine love for you.

Nine in the second place: *Thou wilt keep him in perfect peace whose mind is stayed on thee, because he trusteth in thee* (Isaiah

26:3). Keep your mind in tune with the Infinite. Do not give power to other people. No one can disturb you but yourself. The suggestions, statements and actions of others have no power. The power is the movement of your own thought. Keep your thoughts on God and His Love, and nothing shall hurt you in any manner.

Nine in the third place: . . . *for when I am weak, then am I strong* (II Corinthians 12:10). Never yield to fear. Fear is faith in the wrong thing. Fear is faith upside down. Join up mentally with the God-Presence within you and affirm, "God's Love fills my soul and cleanses my mind. Divine Love goes before me making straight and perfect my way. Divine Love dissolves everything unlike itself."

Six in the fourth place: *There shall no evil befall thee, neither shall any plague come nigh thy dwelling* (Psalms 91:10). *The Lord shall fight for you, and ye shall hold your peace* (Exodus 14:14). Do not resist or wage war in your mind, as this would aggravate the condition. Know that the power and the wisdom resident in your subconscious mind are revealing to you the Divine solution and the happy ending in Divine order.

Nine in the fifth place: . . . *all things work together for good to them that love God* . . . (Romans 8:28). To love God means to give all your allegiance, devotion and loyalty to the one power within you—The Living Spirit Almighty, the Supreme Cause and Power—and to absolutely refuse to give power to any created thing. Know, therefore, that it is God in action in your life, which means all around harmony and peace. Adhere to this truth and blessings will come to you.

Six at the top: *In all thy ways acknowledge him, and he shall direct thy paths* (Proverbs 3:6). *When thou passest through the waters, I will be with thee; and through the rivers, they shall not overflow thee; when thou walkest through the fire, thou shalt not be burned; neither shall the flame kindle upon thee* (Isaiah 43:2).

When depressed or dejected, turn your gaze inward to the God-Presence within you. With faith in God you can move mountains. Love is the fulfilling of the laws of peace, happiness, health and prosperity. Radiate love and goodwill to all. Salute the Divinity in others and wish for them all the blessings of life. As you do, wonders will happen in your life. All good is yours now.

6. SUNG/CONFLICT

**above Ch'ien, The Creative, Heaven**

**below K'an, The Abysmal, Water**

*The Judgment*

*Be not overcome of evil, but overcome evil with good* (Romans 12:21). *And a man's foes shall be they of his own household* (Matthew 10:36). Do not fight or wage war in your mind. Your household is your own mind. The so-called enemy is a negative thought of fear, anger, and hostility in your own mind. Do not act under the sway of a negative emotion. Supplant the negative thoughts with constructive thinking, while claiming Divine guidance and peace of mind. It is to your advantage to seek guidance and spiritual advice.

*The Image*

Realize the harmonizing healing power of God within you is bringing all things to pass in Divine law and order.

*The Lines*

Six at the bottom: *Cast thy burden upon the Lord and he shall sustain thee . . .* (Psalms 55:22). Detach yourself from the problems, tune in with the Infinite, and know that it is God in action in your life bringing harmony, peace and blessings into your life.

Nine in the second place: *Casting all your care upon him, for he careth for you* (I Peter 5:7). Cling steadfastly to the truth that there is a wisdom and a power within you which brings peace where discord is and an abundant supply for every need. When you use mental force or coercion and willpower, you set the law of reversed effort into application and you get the opposite of what you pray for. Stand still and know it is God in action in your life.

Six in the third place: . . . *all things work together for good to them that love God* . . . (Romans 8:28). Realize God is your Employer and that you are working for Him. Salute the Divinity in all your co-workers. Give all honor and glory to God. *How can ye believe, which receive honour one of another and seek not the honour that cometh from God only?* (John 5:44).

Nine in the fourth place: *When he giveth quietness, who then can make trouble?* . . . (Job 34:29). Keep on knowing that there is a Divine harmonious solution through the wisdom and power of God. Let God's peace govern your mind and heart and all will be well.

Nine in the fifth place: . . . *God was with him and delivered him out of all his afflictions* . . . (Acts 7:9-10). There is a happy ending and a wonderful answer to your prayer.

Nine at the top: *Let all your things be done with charity* (I Corinthians 16:14). Our victory must be over our thoughts, feelings, actions and reactions. Discipline yourself so that all your thoughts, images and emotions conform to spiritual standards of whatsoever things are true, lovely, noble and God-like. Where envy and strife are, there is confusion and every evil thing. Your true victory is to fill your soul with God's love and to exercise your dominion over your own thoughts, imagery and emotions and to lead the triumphant life.

## 7. SHIH/THE ARMY

— —

— — **above K'un, The Receptive, Earth**

— —

— —

—— **below K'an, The Abysmal, Water**

— —

*The Judgment*

. . . *Thy faith hath saved thee; go in peace* (Luke 7:50). Your faith and confidence in an Almighty Power to back you up will lead you to victory and triumph over your problems. . . . *if God be for us, who can be against us*? (Romans 8:31). The army represents the multitude of thoughts, ideas, opinions, beliefs and images in your mind. Gather them all together and teach them that there is only One Power—The Living Spirit Almighty—Which flows through your thoughts and images; then you will have a disciplined army. You are here to govern and to control all the people (thoughts) in your mind and to lead them to faith in peace and happiness.

*The Image*

To be a true leader, you must lead the motley crew of your own mind by seeing the truth, hearing only the truth, discerning good from evil, absorbing the spiritual values of life and, finally, incorporating them into your subconscious mind. As you continue to nourish and dwell mentally and emotionally on the eternal verities, they will sink into your subconscious mind and, the law of your subconscious being compulsive, you will be compelled to succeed and to triumph.

*The Lines*

Six at the bottom: *. . . set in order the things that are wanting . . .* (Titus 1:5). It is said that order is heaven's first law. Affirm boldly, "Divine law and order govern all my undertakings, and everything that I seek comes to me in Divine love and in Divine order." When you impress your subconscious with the concept of Divine law and order, you will begin to express yourself at your highest level. Your hidden talents will be revealed, and serenity, peace and harmony will prevail in all phases of your life.

Nine in the second place: *Call unto me and I will answer thee, and shew thee great and mighty things, which thou knowest not* (Jeremiah 33:3). Acknowledge and recognize God as the ruler and guide in your life. As you love and exalt this Supreme Presence within you, giving It supreme allegiance, you will automatically respect and honor the Divinity in others, and you will prosper and grow along all lines.

Six in the third place: *. . . let the dead bury their dead* (Luke 9:60). Don't build cemeteries in your mind. You do that by indulging in grief, sorrow and grudges. If you dig up an old grievance or hurt by rehearsing it in your mind, you are opening a grave in your mind. To think about the past is death. Don't touch mentally any negative thought. Liquidate the past, cremate negative thoughts with the right thoughts, and forget the past. Let Divine love rule in your mind. Your good is this moment. Your future is your present thoughts made manifest.

Six in the fourth place: *Or what king, going to make war against another king, sitteth not down first and consulteth whether he be able with ten thousand to meet him that cometh against him with twenty thousand? . . . he sendeth an ambassage, and desireth conditions of peace* (Luke 14:31–32). If you can't grow a tooth, it is best you go to a dentist and bless him. If you are very ill, see a doctor. If you had the faith you could heal yourself. Don't wait until you get worse. Get immediate attention. According to your faith is it done unto you. Don't blame yourself because you can't meet a certain situation. Do the next best thing and come to a state of peace about it. When the odds seem unsurmountable to you, don't fight the condition; seek counsel and help, and pray for guidance. Remember, if you were always walking in the consciousness of God, you would never be sick and would be able to solve all problems. You have not reached that plateau yet.

If you had no money but you had absolute, unwavering faith that God would supply all your needs, it would be done according to your faith.

Six in the fifth place: . . . *the elder shall serve the younger* (Romans 9:12). You must not permit fear, anger, resentment or vengeance to rule your actions. The elder means the mass mind thinking, early training and indoctrination of false beliefs, prejudices and opinions of others. Your body and environment are the first things you are aware of. Later on you learn about the spiritual values and Presence of God in your depths, and you let wisdom, truth and beauty govern you. This is why the elder (old thoughts) shall now be controlled by the spiritually minded man possessed of true values. If you do not enthrone God's love in your mind and allow yourself to be ruled by it, failure will result. Think good, good follows; think evil, evil follows.

Six at the top: . . . *as a prince hast thou power with God . . .* (Genesis 32:28). You are a prince of God when integrity, honesty and confidence in God reign supreme in your mind and heart. Your decrees are based on eternal verities and the truths of God, which are timeless and changeless. From now on all your ways are pleasantness and all your paths are peace.

## 8. Pi/Holding Together (Union)

— —
—— **above K'an, The Abysmal, Water**
— —
— —
— — **below K'un, The Receptive, Earth**
— —

*The Judgment*

*. . . if thou wilt enter into life, keep the commandments* (Matthew 19:17). Adhere strictly to honesty, integrity and justice. Do not deviate from that course which deep in your heart you know is the right one to follow.

*The Image*

*Let your light so shine before men, that they may see your good works, and glorify your father which is in heaven* (Matthew 5:16). As you exalt God in the midst of you, so too will you automatically exalt God in all those around you, thereby contributing to the harmony, peace and prosperity of all members of your family and your associates.

*The Lines*

Six at the bottom: *. . . let us not love in word, neither in tongue; but in deed and in truth* (I John 3:18). Love is an outpouring of the heart; it is impersonal goodwill to all. While you maintain this attitude, the law of attraction will work for you and bring you countless blessings along all lines and with surprising promptness.

Six in the second place: *A good man out of the good treasure of the heart bringeth forth good things . . .* (Matthew 12:35). As you continue to exude vibrancy and goodwill to all, your success and prosperity are assured.

Six in the third place: *He that troubleth his own house shall inherit the wind . . .* (Proverbs 11:29). The house is your mind. Be sure you entertain only thoughts of harmony, health, peace, joy and goodwill. If you associate in your mind with thoughts based on eternal verities, you will not associate with people who do not conform to your spiritual standards. Choose your friends only as they conform to these spiritual criteria.

Six in the fourth place: *Let your speech be always with grace, seasoned with salt, that ye may know how ye ought to answer every man* (Colossians 4:6). You have to taste salt to get its savor. Symbolically, to have salt means you must have zeal, enthusiasm and an inner joy which makes life far more palatable and more vital. This inner feeling of yours is contagious and is communicated to all those around you, bringing expansion and growth into all phases of your life.

Nine in the fifth place: *The desire of the righteous shall be granted* (Proverbs 10:24). Know that Divine right action is operating on your behalf and you can be assured of success and victory.

Six at the top: *For where two or three are gathered together in my name, there am I in the midst of them* (Matthew 18:20). To fulfill your desires and aspirations, continuous harmony and agreement are essential. In other words, your dominant conviction must be based on Divine law and order, since confusion in your mind would lead to loss and failure.

## 9. Hsiao Ch'u/The Taming Power of the Small

——
—— **above Sun, The Gentle, Wind**
— —
——
—— **below Ch'ien, The Creative, Heaven**
——

*The Judgment*

*The Lord is my shepherd; I shall not want* (Psalms 23:1). The Lordly Power—the God-Presence within you—is watching over you, and you shall not want for evidence of the fact that God is guiding you and fulfilling all your needs now.

*The Image*

*The Lord stood with me and strengthened me . . .* (II Timothy 4:17). Continue to live in faith and confidence and you will advance, grow and move forward along all lines.

*The Lines*

Nine at the bottom: . . . *no good thing will be withheld from them that walk uprightly* (Psalms 84:11). Keep in tune with the Infinite. You can rest assured that you will achieve, accomplish and bring to pass the most cherished desires of your heart.

Nine in the second place: . . . *God was with him, and delivered him out of all his afflictions . . .* (Acts 7:9–10). Do not try to force things. Relax, let go and trust Infinite Intelligence to bring things to pass in the right way at the right time.

Nine in the third place: *And if a house be divided against itself, that house cannot stand* (Mark 3:25). The house is your mind. When you are confused or angry in your mind, things do not work out well. Calm your emotions. Get back on the beam.

Six in the fourth place: *When he giveth quietness who then can make trouble? . . .* (Job 34:29). Do not give power to others. No one has the power to disturb you or to hurt you except through your own thoughts. Give all power to the God-Presence within you and know all things are working out in Divine order, and all fear will then vanish from your mind.

Nine in the fifth place: *Thou wilt keep him in perfect peace whose mind is stayed on thee . . .* (Isaiah 26:3). As you exalt God in the midst of you, all your associates will feel your vibration and enthusiasm, and all of you will prosper.

Nine at the top: *God is my strength and power, and he maketh my way perfect* (II Samuel 22:33). There is a time for everything under the sun. Rest and let go. Trust Infinite Intelligence to bring all things to pass at the right time in the right way.

## 10. Lü/Treading (Conduct)

——

—— **above Ch'ien, The Creative, Heaven**

——

— —

—— **below Tui, The Joyous, Lake**

——

*The Judgment*

*Pleasant words are as an honeycomb, sweet to the soul, and health to the bones* (Proverbs 16:24). A soft answer turneth away wrath. You would not be angry with a man who is a hunchback or otherwise crippled. You would have compassion on him. Many individuals are mental hunchbacks with warped and distorted minds. Bless them and walk on. Good fortune is yours.

*The Image*

*Let us therefore follow after the things which make for peace, and things wherewith one may edify another* (Romans 14:19). Choose your thoughts carefully. Practice discernment. Separate the chaff from the wheat in your mind. Salute the Divinity within yourself while realizing that every man is an epitome of the Divine, and good will come to you.

*The Lines*

Nine at the bottom: *They that seek the Lord shall not want any good thing* (Psalms 34:10). Acknowledge the God-Presence within you as your senior partner and know that the inner felicity of your heart meets with kindness and goodwill everywhere and is subjectively felt by others. There is a happy outcome to your experiences.

Nine in the second place: Shakespeare spoke eloquently when he had Polonius state, "To thine own self be true; then it follows, as the night the day, thou canst not be false to any man." Remain true to your ideals and goals in life and all that you do will prosper.

Six in the third place: *The legs of the lame are not equal; so is a parable in the mouth of fools* (Proverbs 26:7). . . . *if therefore thine eye be single, thy whole body shall be full of light* (Matthew 6:22). This means that you give your attention to the God-Presence within you, and that you place the glory and power of God first in your life; then do you become a channel for the Divine and your eye is single and your whole embodiment becomes full of light and love.

A parable has two sides: there is an inner and an outer meaning which correspond. Your inner mood or feeling controls your external world. Don't blame others; do not let others irritate you. Realize your boss is your Higher Self (God) and submit to the law of goodness, truth and beauty within you, and nothing will hurt you. If you hold resentment and permit yourself to be emotionally disturbed, you will experience loss in many ways. . . . *In quietness and in confidence shall be your strength* . . . (Isaiah 30:15).

Nine in the fourth place: . . . *be careful to maintain good works* . . . (Titus 3:8). Do nothing of a foolhardy nature. Use ordinary caution and common sense in all your undertakings. Know that you can accomplish all things through the God-Power which strengthens you.

Nine in the fifth place: *Discretion shall preserve thee, understanding shall keep thee* (Proverbs 2:11). Be alert, on the *qui vive*. Make sure your decisions are wise. To have understanding is to know a way out of trouble and to know how to live in peace and harmony on this planet. Know that Infinite Intelligence guides and directs you in all your undertakings and that you are watched over by an Overshadowing Presence at all times.

Nine at the top: *For by me thy days shall be multiplied, and the years of thy life shall be increased* (Proverbs 9:11). When your thoughts are wise, your actions will be wise. When your attitude is right and you live in the expectancy of the best, invariably the best will come to you. Success and prosperity are yours now.

## 11. T'AI/PEACE

\- - 
\- - **above K'un, The Receptive, Earth**
\- - 
——
—— **below Ch'ien, The Creative, Heaven**
——

### *The Judgment*

*Thou wilt keep him in perfect peace whose mind is stayed on thee* . . . (Isaiah 26:3). Keep your mind stayed upon the Spiritual Presence within you. When your mind is at peace and in tune with the Infinite, you will find peace in your home, business, and in all aspects of your life. Furthermore, you will prosper beyond your fondest dreams.

### *The Image*

. . . *if two of you shall agree on earth as touching anything that they shall ask, it shall be done for them of my Father which is in heaven* (Matthew 18:19). This means that when your conscious and subconscious agree, the Creative Power (The Father) brings your desire to pass. When there is an agreement in your conscious and subconscious mind and both synchronize and unite on your ideal and goal, you will experience the joy of the answered prayer.

### *The Lines*

Nine at the bottom: . . . *and whatsoever he doeth shall prosper* (Psalms 1:3). To prosper means to grow and expand along all lines

—spiritually, mentally, materially and financially. The law of attraction is now working for you and you attract all those who will aid and assist you in the attainment of your goals.

Nine in the second place: . . . *strait is the gate, and narrow is the way, which leadeth unto life, and few there be that find it* (Matthew 7:14). It is only by a change in your mental attitude that outer conditions can be altered. This is called the straight gate, the royal road of the ancients, the middle path of Buddha. In order to bring harmony, peace, prosperity and health into your experience, there is only one way, and that is to impregnate your subconscious vith thoughts of harmony, peace, abundance and security.

Don't give power to others or to externals. Refuse to recognize the false beliefs of the mass mind, such as belief in the power of the stars, evil entities, predestination, karma, fate, etc. Give all power to God within you and walk the earth with faith and confidence in the One Power and Cause, and you will win and triumph along all lines.

Nine in the third place: There is an old maxim in life: "This, too, shall pass away." Everything changes into its opposite. You can lead a balanced, creative life without experiencing the great cycles of ups and downs by affirming boldly: "Divine law and order govern my entire life and Divine right action governs me at all times." You want just enough variation in life to make it interesting. Many swing from exhilaration to depression, from feeling good to feeling blue. You can be happy on a rainy day as well as on a sunny day. Watch your mental and spiritual climate. This determines all your experiences in life. Enjoy the mood of success and achievement and rest assured of victory.

Six in the fourth place: . . . *these ought ye to have done, and not to leave the other undone* (Luke 11:42). You must be very careful how you help a person. You *leave the other undone* when you do not give him the wisdom or the know-how to tap the powers of his subconscious mind. When he becomes aware of these powers he will never want a hand-out or a bowl of soup or an old suit of clothes again. Life's lesson is that each of us must learn to stand on his own feet, meeting and overcoming his personal problems and challenges. Help given too easily denies and robs the man of true self-esteem and self-propulsion. Teach a man his Divinity and the Source of wealth, then you will have given him the know-how and you will not have left the other half of the equation undone. Help him, yes, but make sure you don't let him lean on you. Teach him to lean on God and he will always be cared for.

Six in the fifth place: . . . *what therefore God hath joined together, let not man put asunder* (Matthew 19:6). God is love, and when love unites two hearts, they beat in unison and harmony. Marriage for any other reason would not be a marriage but a sham, a farce and a masquerade. A marriage (psychologically speaking) can also be a business contract or partnership or professional affiliation. All such agreements should be based on mutual goodwill and harmony, and should be agreeable and satisfactory to each person. From this harmonious agreement, success and happiness are assured.

Six at the top: . . . *resist not evil, but whosoever shall smite thee on thy right cheek, turn to him the other also* (Matthew 5:39). This is the secret of success and happiness in life. When you resist mentally any undesirable or unpleasant condition, you endow it with more power, which automatically makes matters worse for you. Don't hurl yourself against the condition mentally. Refrain from resisting the trouble mentally. Contemplate God in action in your life and understand that the Divine law of harmony is operating in your behalf and in all those around you, and you will find the problem fades away and you are free. This is the true meaning of *loving your enemy*, which confuses so many people. It is superb mental strategy. Try it and you will win.

## 12. P'I/STANDSTILL (STAGNATION)

——<br>
—— **above Ch'ien, The Creative, Heaven**<br>
——<br>
– –<br>
– – **below K'un, The Receptive, Earth**<br>
– –

### *The Judgment*

*The fear of the wicked, it shall come upon him; but the desire of the righteous shall be granted* (Proverbs 10:24). . . . *he is a buckler to all them that trust in him* (II Samuel 22:31). Adhere to the principles of truth and do not permit anyone to cause you to deviate from the principles of harmony, health and peace. Be still and quiet and trust the law of harmony to bring all things to pass in Divine order.

### *The Image*

Having set your ideals, remain true to them in spite of anger, criticism and vituperation. Remain steadfastly true to your inner code and pattern of life based on goodness, honesty and integrity. Know also that what is right action for you must of necessity be right action for all based on the principle of right action. Let no one dissuade you or switch you off onto side tracks regardless of their arguments and persuasions to the contrary.

### *The Lines*

Six at the bottom: . . . *whosoever trusteth in the Lord, happy is he* (Proverbs 16:20). Place your confidence and trust in the Supreme Intelligence within you, which is your Higher Self. It is interested in your welfare and spiritual expansion. Keep on knowing that God loves you and cares for you and that Infinite Spirit is watching over you, revealing to you the next step in your unfoldment. This is a time for meditation and prayer, which will be followed by happiness and success.

Six in the second place: . . . *meddle not with him that flattereth* . . . (Proverbs 20:19). Pay no attention to sycophants or idle flattery. Adhere strictly to the spiritual values of life which are eternal and never change. Continue to make the acquiring of wisdom a passion, and great and mighty things will enrich your life, and you will experience the peace that passeth understanding.

Six in the third place: *For whosoever exalteth himself shall be abased* . . . (Luke 14:11). A man who employs devious means, trickery or what he calls pull to get ahead is misusing the law of his subconscious by exalting himself the *wrong* way. Because his subconscious is aware of his inferiority, guilt and sense of lack, he will be forced to step down from the position he acquired in the wrong way. It is well known in political, business and professional fields that the more you push and strive to advance yourself externally, the quicker will you bring on your downfall. Man promotes himself by establishing the mental equivalent of success, integrity, zeal and enthusiasm in his subconscious mind, which then compels him to rise. In other words, man promotes himself by his mental attitude or state of consciousness.

Nine in the fourth place: *But there is a spirit in man, and the inspiration of the Almighty giveth them understanding* (Job 32:8). God is the highest and greatest authority and the greatest wisdom. It is the Supreme Spirit within you. It is All-Wise, the Ever-Living One and the All-Knowing One. Call on this Inner Power and you will be inspired and guided to do the right thing. You will prosper and succeed and bless all those associated with you.

Nine in the fifth place: *Wisdom strengtheneth the wise more than ten mighty men which are in the city* (Ecclesiastes 7:19). Wisdom is an awareness of the Presence and Power of God within you. Join up with this God-Presence within you, knowing that . . . *they that wait upon the Lord shall renew their strength; they shall mount up with wings as eagles; they shall run, and not be weary; and they shall walk, and not faint* (Isaiah 40:31).

Know that the Power of the Almighty is moving on your behalf and that there is nothing to oppose Omnipotence. With this attitude, you will rise victoriously over all problems. The word "wait" in the Bible means quieting the mind and calling upon the Infinite Power, which responds and becomes active and potent in one's life. The Infinite cannot fail. There is nothing to oppose It, thwart It or vitiate It. It is all powerful.

Nine at the top: *Be still and know that I am God . . .* (Psalms 46:10). This means to quiet your mind and know that your own "I-AM-NESS" is God and that when you say "I AM" you are announcing the Presence of God within you—Pure Being, the Self-Originating Intelligence, unconditioned consciousness, awareness, the Life-Principle. The name of God is the nature of God, as God has no name. As you realize and give recognition to God in action in your life, you will find everything changing into order and harmony. Everything negative in your life passes away and you will experience the many blessings of life.

## 13. T'UNG JEN/FELLOWSHIP WITH MEN

——
—— **above Ch'ien, The Creative, Heaven**
——
——
— — **below Li, The Clinging, Flame**
——

*The Judgment*

*. . . for the Lord thy God, he it is that doth go with thee; he will not fail thee, nor forsake thee* (Deuteronomy 31:6). Intend your

mind vigorously and confidently in the direction of a greater and larger experience. Cross from where you are in your mind to a new place, job, assignment or location in your mind. Your mind is called water in the Bible, and you cross the water when you move mentally from where you are to a mental acceptance of what you want to be, to do, or to have. Prayer is a mental journey to the promised land, or to the realization of your heart's desire. If this entails a journey to Hawaii or any other place, take it and rejoice in the fulfillment of your dream. You will prosper.

*The Image*

*Commit thy way unto the Lord; trust also in him and he shall bring it to pass* (Psalms 37:5). Radiate love and goodwill to all. Establish your goal and purpose, and the law of affinity will attract to you all those who will aid you in the fulfillment of your desire Divine wisdom governs you and you will be guided aright.

*The Lines*

Nine at the bottom: *The steps of a good man are ordered by the Lord; and he delighteth in his way* (Psalms 37:23). Honesty, sincerity, candor and goodwill govern all your undertakings, and the camaraderie of the Spirit prevails, blessing all concerned.

Six in the second place: *He that loveth his brother abideth in the light, and there is none occasion of stumbling in him* (I John 2:10). There must be no ill will, bigotry or prejudice governing your decisions. Your motivations, actions and decisions must be based on goodwill to all; otherwise, you attract loss and limitation.

Nine in the third place: *And when ye stand praying, forgive, if ye have aught against any . . .* (Mark 11:25). . . . *forgive, and ye shall be forgiven* (Luke 6:37). . . . *vengeance is mine; I will repay, saith the Lord* (Romans 12:19). You can't afford to harbor ill will or resentment, or seek to get even with someone else. Remember, you are the one thinking and feeling the hostility. This mental attitude robs you of vitality, enthusiasm, energy, and leaves you a physical and mental wreck. Release the other mentally, bless him and walk on. If another is doing something wrong, the law of his own mind takes care of him. What you wish for another, you wish for yourself. Get the other one out of your hair by surrendering him to God and wishing for him all the blessings of life. As you do this, you will eradicate the sting in your mind.

Nine in the fourth place: . . . *if we love one another, God dwelleth in us* . . . (I John 4:12). Realize the Presence of God in the other and claim that harmony, peace and understanding reign supreme, and you will experience success and peace of mind.

Nine in the fifth place: . . . *for out of the abundance of the heart the mouth speaketh. A good man out of the good treasure of the heart bringeth forth good things* . . . (Matthew 12:34–35). When two hearts beat as one, unity, harmony and understanding exist between them. The law of attraction brings them together in Divine order and they accomplish great things together.

Nine at the top: . . . *walk in love* . . . (Ephesians 5:2). Love means an outreaching of the heart, i.e., goodwill to all men. Exude vibrancy and salute the Divinity in all those you meet. The past is dead. Nothing lives but this moment. Change your present thoughts and keep them changed, and you change your destiny. *Remember ye not the former things, neither consider the things of old* (Isaiah 43:18).

## 14. Ta Yu/Possession in Great Measure

——
— — **above Li, The Clinging, Flame**
——
——
—— **below Ch'ien, The Creative, Heaven**
——

*The Judgment*

*. . . the Lord thy God shall bless thee in all thine increase, and in all the works of thine hands, therefore thou shalt surely rejoice* (Deuteronomy 16:15). Whatever you do will excel in a magnificent way.

*The Image*

*The mouth of the righteous speaketh wisdom . . .* (Psalms 37:30). Wisdom is the conscious awareness of the presence and power of God within you. Give all power to God—the Supreme Intelligence within you—and absolutely refuse to give any power to negative thoughts or to any person, place or thing. Aspire only to what is lovely and of good report.

*The Lines*

Nine at the bottom: *For God hath not given us the spirit of fear, but of power, and of love, and of a sound mind* (II Timothy 1:7). Fear is indicative of a lack of faith in God. Fear is faith in that which is false. Refuse to indulge negative thoughts of any kind. Supplant them at once with faith in God and all good things.

Nine in the second place: *Cast thy burden upon the Lord and he shall sustain thee . . .* (Psalms 55:22). Find the rock of strength within yourself. The Kingdom of God is within you; you will find It a tower of strength as you become conscious of It. This Infinite Power continuously moves through you and all those connected with you, and this Power enables you to transcend all barriers in the accomplishment of your purposes.

Nine in the third place: *. . . as having nothing, and yet possessing all things* (II Corinthians 6:10). God possesses all things. You are a steward of the Divine, and you should use your talents and riches wisely, judiciously and constructively. Recognize God as the Source of your supply and give all honor and glory to the Source of all blessings. The rich young man spoken of in the Book of Mark, Chapter 10, was a man rich in preconceived opinions, false beliefs about God, life and the universe. His mind was cluttered with false beliefs about disease, and was afflicted with lack and limitation of all kinds. Divest yourself of all false beliefs and false dogma and believe . . . *in the living God, who giveth us richly all things to enjoy* (I Timothy 6:17).

Nine in the fourth place: *Let all your things be done with charity* (I Corinthians 16:14). . . . *charity envieth not* . . . (I Corinthians 13:4). Wish success and happiness for everyone. You are unique, there is no one in all the world like you, as God never repeats Himself. Realize that God is the Source of all things and that you can go within yourself, claim your wealth, and your subconscious will respond accordingly. You receive nothing except by right of consciousness. (You must possess the mental equivalent of it.)

Six in the fifth place: . . . *by love serve one another* (Galatians 5:13). If you serve others through love you serve yourself as well, and you will prosper accordingly.

Nine in the sixth place: . . . *turn not from it to the right hand or to the left, that thou mayest prosper whithersoever thou goest* (Joshua 1:7). This means not to give any power to the objective world (right hand) or to the left (belief in fate, power of the past, karma or entities), but to give all power to the God-Self within you, while knowing that the Living Spirit is moving on your behalf, and you will experience thereby countless blessings, and whatsoever you do will prosper.

## 15. Ch'ien/Modesty

— —
— — **above K'un, The Receptive, Earth**
— —
——
— — **below Ken, Keeping Still, Mountain**
— —

*The Judgment*

*Put on therefore . . . humbleness of mind . . .* (Colossians 3:12). *. . . before honour is humility* (Proverbs 15:33). Humility means you are teachable, open minded and receptive to the truths of God; growth, expansion and achievement follow naturally. The great men of the world are humble. Real humility values the truth above all things and is ever ready to receive it. The reward of humility is riches, honor and life more abundant.

*The Image*

*Blessed are the meek: for they shall inherit the earth* (Matthew 5:5). The "earth" means your body and all the manifestations of your life, such as your business, your home, your profession and experiences. All these are expressions of inner mental attitudes. The word "meek," Biblically speaking, means a person who gives all power and glory to God and who realizes that the will of God for all men is something wonderful, joyous, fascinating and transcending our fondest dreams. This is the key to health, happiness, abundance and security.

*The Lines*

Six at the bottom: *The way of life is above to the wise . . .* (Proverbs 15:24). *And he said, let us take our journey, and let us go, and I will go before thee* (Genesis 33:12). Make a decision, travel from where you are in your mind to that point in life which you want to attain. Nourish that decision, envelop it in faith and confidence, and it will come to pass. You have crossed the waters of your mind, and any external journey over water or land will bless you.

Six in the second place: *. . . and the Lord wrought a great victory* (II Samuel 23:12). The Lord is the power of your subconscious mind which is now expressing what you have impressed upon it, and you are growing spiritually, mentally and materially. Success and victory are assured.

Nine in the third place: *Thou shalt also decree a thing, and it shall be established unto thee* (Job 22:28). Maintain feelingly and knowingly that all good is yours. You will bring the desire of your heart to fruition.

Six in the fourth place: *For every man shall bear his own burden* (Galatians 6:5). You have to do your share in life by putting your shoulder to the wheel and contributing your talents for the benefit of humanity. Stand on your own feet, meet your problems, and through the power of God you will succeed. You are part of humanity and you are here to serve and give life to your talents by contributing to the peace and happiness of humanity.

Six in the fifth place: *Be not overcome of evil, but overcome evil with good* (Romans 12:21). Note that Paul uses the words "of evil," i.e., do not permit negative thoughts to lodge in your mind and govern you. Cremate them with spiritual thoughts and Divine love. Look for the Presence of God in your associates, and if you see faults, imagine that they have the corresponding virtues. Dwelling on the faults of others causes you to build them into your own mentality. Exalt God in the midst of you and everything you do will bless and benefit not only you but countless others.

Six in the sixth place: *Let nothing be done through strife or vainglory . . . Look not every man on his own things, but every man also on the things of others* (Philippians 2:3,4). The vainglorious person is always humiliated. Modesty is freedom from boastfulness, braggadocio and vanity. Simplicity and moderation in all things characterize the modest man. He respects and has regard for decency of behavior and speech. The modest man has humility, and he does all things for the glory of God. Discipline your thoughts and emotions, and when your attention wanders away, bring it back to the contemplation of His Holy Presence; then you can be assured of victory and success in all your undertakings.

## 16. YU/ENTHUSIASM

— —<br>
— — **above Chen, The Arousing, Thunder**<br>
——<br>
— —<br>
— — **below K'un, The Receptive, Earth**<br>
— —

### *The Judgment*

*And thou shalt have joy and gladness . . .* (Luke 1:14). Enthusiasm means to be possessed by God. When you have an absorbing or a lively interest in some project, cause or subject, i.e., when you are fired with the idea and have gladness in your heart, you are bound to succeed. Moreover, your enthusiastic mood will be communicated to others, as enthusiasm is contagious.

### *The Image*

*Let your light so shine before men, that they may see your good works, and glorify your Father which is in heaven* (Matthew 5:16). You glorify God, the Father of all, when you become a channel of the Divine and you let His intelligence, wisdom, love, harmony and abundance flow through you. To sacrifice is to make sacred; i.e., you dedicate all your work to God, knowing that you are directed and governed over by a Divine wisdom. As you practice this, you will find all your ways are pleasantness and all your paths are peace.

### *The Lines*

Six at the bottom: *For by grace are ye saved through faith . . . not of works, lest any man should boast* (Ephesians 2:8,9) The law of your subconscious is absolutely just and eminently fair. Grace is the response of your deeper mind to your habitual thinking and imagery. Your experiences, status in life, wealth and position are a mathematical and exact reproduction of your belief and inner conviction. Do not brag or boast. You are what you contemplate, and there is no use pretending to be what you do not feel in your heart is true. You are always demonstrating your beliefs and assumptions. Get a higher vision and know that through the power of God you can reach it. You go where your vision is. Man is belief expressed. Your faith in the laws of your mind must be demonstrated, otherwise it is not true faith.

Six in the second place: *And the rain descended, and the floods came and the winds blew, and beat upon the house; and it fell not; for it was founded upon a rock* (Matthew 7:25). The rock represents that which is impregnable, invisible and impervious to all external forces. The house is your mind where your thoughts, feelings, beliefs and opinions dwell. You have absolute faith in the God-Power Which is Supreme and Omnipotent, and with this faith no one can cause you to doubt or deviate from your aim or goal. Faith is confidence in the Supreme Power Which responds through your subconscious mind and brings the cherished desires of your heart to pass. Success is assured you.

Six in the third place: *A double minded man is unstable in all his ways* (James 1:8). You must be ready to accept the opportunity when it comes. If a project looks good to you, accept it and pronounce it good, and claim it is God in action in your life. When you hesitate, procrastinate, vacillate and waver, you lose the opportunity to move forward. Trust God to guide you in all your ways. Be alert and on the *qui vive*, and realize that opportunity is always knocking at your door.

Nine in the fourth place: *Call unto me, and I will answer thee, and shew thee great and mighty things, which thou knowest not* (Jeremiah 33:3). As you keep looking to the Inner Source of all blessings, knowing that God is guiding you and prospering you in all ways, you will discover that new creative ideas come to you from your subliminal depths, and you will advance beyond your fondest dreams.

Six in the fifth place: *The Spirit of God hath made me, and the breath of the Almighty hath given me life* (Job 33:4). God is life and that is your life now. God is the Life-Principle in you. Affirm boldly and with feeling, "I inhale the peace of God and I exhale the love of God to all, for I know that love is the fulfilling of the law of health, happiness, peace and abundance." God in the midst of you is healing you now. . . . *I am the Lord that healeth thee* (Exodus 15:26).

Six in the sixth place: *Thou shalt remember the Lord thy God, for it is he that giveth thee power to get wealth* (Deuteronomy 8:18). Look always to the Source of supply. Control yourself so that neither the ups nor downs of life are too accented. Guard your moods and always maintain a balance. You need enough variation to make life interesting. Know that Divine law and order govern you at all times, and you will not go too far either way. God's river of peace governs you and all will be well.

## 17. Sui/Following

– –
—— **above Tui, The Joyous, Lake**
——
– –
– – **below Chen, The Arousing, Thunder**
——

*The Judgment*

. . . *but he that shall endure unto the end, the same shall be saved* (Mark 13:13). The word "saved" means a solution to your problem; and if you persist in right thinking and right feeling, you will get a response from your subconscious mind and your prayer will be answered. Perseverance, tenacity and determination in pursuing that which is good and that which blesses you and others will cause it inevitably to come to pass.

*The Image*

*The Lord shall guide thee continually* . . . (Isaiah 58:11). Plan to have regular sessions during the day for communing with the Divine Presence. Turn to the Indwelling God and claim guidance, power, strength and wisdom to govern all your decisions and actions, and your labors will be blessed. Charge your mental and spiritual batteries regularly and systematically.

*The Lines*

Nine at the bottom: *The steps of a good man are ordered by the Lord; and he delighteth in his way* (Psalms 37:23). Realize and know that Divine right action governs you and exude vibrancy and goodwill to all, and you will find the cooperation and assistance you need to fulfill your purposes.

Six in the second place: . . . *I am the Lord thy God which teacheth thee to profit, which leadeth thee by the way that thou shouldest go* (Isaiah 48:17). In business or whatever profession you may follow, claim that all those connected with you are spiritual links in the chain of your growth, welfare and prosperity. All your associates should be chosen based on spiritual criteria; i.e., those who have a reverence for things Divine. Put God first in your life and continuously give all honor and glory to God, and then you will automatically do the right thing.

Six in the third place: . . . *the way of the righteous is made plain* (Proverbs 15:19). Think right, feel right, act right, be right. Think, speak and act from the standpoint of the Infinite Principle of Harmony within you. To succeed in life, you must give up the lesser for the greater. You are here to grow, to rise and transcend life's problems. Walk with the highest and the best mentally and every other way, and you will invariably experience the best.

Nine in the fourth place: *And thine ears shall hear a word behind thee, saying, This is the way, walk ye in it* . . . (Isaiah 30:21). Take command of your mind. Adhere to that which you know to be true.

Preserve your equanimity and rest with absolute assurance that the Infinite Presence is moving on your behalf. Your motivation must be for the benefit of all. Listen to what the Psalmist said and obey it: *They speak vanity everyone with his neighbour: with flattering lips and with a double heart do they speak* (Psalms 12:2). Listen to the inner voice of the Divine, which always speaks in peace, in love and in harmony.

Nine in the fifth place: . . . *He maketh my way perfect* (II Samuel 22:33). Integrate yourself around the conviction of God's guidance and the expectancy of the best, and you will reap a rich harvest.

Six in the sixth place: *God is my strength and power, and he maketh my way perfect* (II Samuel 22:33). Look for spiritual help and all kinds of assistance from those only who have a reverence for the Divinity which shapes our ends. As you lead so will they follow.

## 18. KU/WORK ON WHAT HAS BEEN SPOILED (DECAY)

———<br>
— — **above Ken, Keeping Still, Mountain**<br>
— —<br>
———<br>
——— **below Sun, The Gentle, Wind**<br>
— —

*The Judgment*

. . . *he walked on the water, to go to Jesus* (Matthew 14:29). One of the meanings of Jesus as He is portrayed in the Bible is the realization of your heart's desire which would save you from your current predicament. If hungry, food would be your savior; if thirsty, water would be your savior; if in prison, freedom would be your savior; and if sick, health would be your savior. Symbolically, water means your mind, and it is to your advantage to intend your mind in the direction of a larger expresson across the waters of your mind within yourself. Take up a new residence in your mind, which means nourish a new decision, sustain it with faith, and if it involves outer travel, by all means take the trip. The inner controls the outer. Accept the new opportunity. As you begin with faith and confidence, the end result will be successful in all ways. The beginning and the end are one.

*The Image*

*In all thy ways acknowledge him, and he will make plain thy paths* (Proverbs 3:6). When you assert a truth, such as the above, knowing that it is God in action in your life, you will be lifted up and inspired, and all obstructions will be removed. Your uplifted spirit will be communicated to others, and they will aid you in the realization of your plans.

*The Lines*

Six at the bottom: . . . *and I will raise up the decayed places thereof* (Isaiah 44:26). Nothing is forever. Everything changes. The past is dead. Nothing matters but this moment. Change this moment and you change your destiny. There is no occasion to grieve over the mistakes of the past. The future is your present thinking made manifest. You will reap a rich harvest as you sow God-like thoughts in the garden of your mind now.

Nine in the second place: . . . *Now is the day of salvation* (II Corinthians 6:2). Live in the present. Prepare wisely for the future and let the past alone. Salvation means that right now God has the answer, the solution. It is foolish to waste your energy on the dead past. Think good and good follows. See God in all those around you and wish for them health, happiness and peace, and good will come to you.

Nine in the third place: *For whosoever shall call upon the name of the Lord shall be saved* (Romans 10:13). Revise all your thinking and creedal beliefs, and make sure they conform to eternal verities. There is no time or space in mind. The moment you begin to think constructively and wisely, there is an immediate and automatic reaction from your subconscious mind. The past mistakes and errors are wiped out in the same manner as errors in the chemical laboratory are wiped out when you begin to use the principles of chemistry correctly. Forget the past and blame no one. You mold and fashion your own destiny by your thought and feeling.

Six in the fourth place: *Remember ye not the former things, neither consider the things of old* (Isaiah 43:18). Never accept false beliefs or outmoded dogmas which are illogical, unreasonable and unscientific. Accept ideas and truths which heal, bless, inspire, dignify and elevate you. To indulge in the past and the false beliefs and traditions of the past will bring loss, lack and limitation into your life.

Six in the fifth place: . . . *they that seek the Lord shall not want any good thing* (Psalms 34:10). State the truth that all good is yours and it will become manifest in your affairs. You will be guided in all ways. Infinite Intelligence of your subconscious will attract to you all those who will aid you in the realization of your dreams and aspirations.

Nine in the sixth place: *There is a spirit in man; and the inspiration of the Almighty giveth them understanding* (Job 32:8). When you are inspired from On High, you will find your true expression in life, and you will do what you love to do. Whatever you say, do, write or create can only bless mankind in countless ways. You will be a true channel of Divine wisdom.

## 19. Lin/Approach

— —<br>
— — **above K'un, The Receptive, Earth**<br>
— —<br>
— —<br>
——— **below Tui, The Joyous, Lake**<br>
———

*The Judgment*

*He shall call upon me and I will answer him. I will be with him in trouble: I will deliver him and honour him* (Psalms 91:15). *When the enemy shall come in like a flood, the Spirit of the Lord shall lift up a standard against him* (Isaiah 59:19). As you keep in tune with the Infinite, you will advance and move forward along all lines. When you call upon Infinite Intelligence, It responds according to the nature of your request. Do not indulge in fear, worry, anger or resentment in your mind, as these negative emotions bring loss and limitation. Fill your mind with the concepts of love, faith and confidence, and you will eradicate the negatives. Remember, all the water in the sea can't sink a ship unless the water gets inside the ship. Likewise, negative thoughts, or the actions of others can't hurt you except you indulge them in your mind. Cremate them; burn them up with Divine Love.

*The Image*

*But my God shall supply all your need according to his riches in glory . . .* (Philippians 4:19). All the energy, vitality, wisdom, power, and strength you need are given to you freely. God is your instant and everlasting supply and support, and the more wisdom you give the more you receive. You can't exhaust the Infinite Treasure House within you.

*The Lines*

Nine at the bottom: *And all things, whatsoever ye shall ask in prayer, believing, ye shall receive* (Matthew 21:22). Believe the great truth that all good is unfolding for you and it will become a visible possession.

Nine in the second place: *God giveth to a man that is good in his sight wisdom, and knowledge, and joy . . .* (Ecclesiastes 2:26). Nothing moves you, nothing disturbs you, nothing worries you, because you are sustained by these words: "This, too, shall pass away." Everything passes away but God, and God alone is sufficient. God gives you all the wisdom, power and creative ideas you need to fulfill your plans, and everything you do will prosper.

Six in the third place: *. . . be careful to maintain good works . . .* (Titus 3:8). If you are negligent in your mind and permit negative emotions to govern you, whatever you do will not go well. You can't afford to be careless and indifferent in your mind. You must keep prayed up, otherwise the mass mind will govern you with thoughts of fear, lack, worry and anxiety. Change your thoughts and keep them changed.

Six in the fourth place: *. . . who is this that engaged his heart to approach unto me? saith the Lord* (Jeremiah 30:21). Your heart is the seat of emotions and of love. As you turn to the God-Presence within you, full of faith and confidence, everything you do will prosper.

Six in the fifth place: *The Lord will perfect that which concerneth me . . .* (Psalms 138:8). Your appreciation and recognition of the Lordly Power within you will bring all things to pass in Divine order.

Six in the sixth place: *Surely goodness and mercy shall follow me all the days of my life: and I will dwell in the house of the Lord forever* (Psalms 23:6). Sensing your oneness with God and with all men, you exude vibrancy, love and goodwill to all, and all those whom you contact are blessed because you walk this way.

## 20. KUAN/CONTEMPLATION (VIEW)

———
——— **above Sun, The Gentle, Wind**
— —
— —
— — **below K'un, The Receptive, Earth**
— —

*The Judgment*

*Call unto me, and I will answer thee, and shew thee great and mighty things which thou knowest not* (Jeremiah 33:3). Man is that which he contemplates. Whatever you contemplate takes form and expression in your life. A sacrifice as found in the Bible means to give up the lesser for the greater, i.e., to substitute a constructive thought for a negative one. As you recognize the supremacy and sovereignty of the Spirit within you and call upon It for guidance, the answer will come to you in Divine order.

*The Image*

*In all thy ways acknowledge him and he will make plain thy paths* (Proverbs 3:6). As you recognize the truth that God is an ever present help at all times and as you claim that you are inspired and directed to say and do the right thing, you will discover that whatever you say and do will be right for the occasion.

*The Lines*

Six at the bottom: *If any man among you seem to be religious, and bridleth not his tongue, but deceiveth his own heart, this man's religion is vain* (James 1:26). You must realize that there are principles and truths which never vary. They are the same yesterday, today and forever. Sincerity and honesty in religion are essential, and it is necessary to conform to the truths of life. What you affirm must be *felt* as true in your heart. Lip service to eternal verities is meaningless.

Six in the second place: . . . *if therefore thine eye be single, thy whole body shall be full of light* (Matthew 6:22). Whatever you direct your attention to will come into your experience in a material way. Avoid narrow-minded, constricted viewpoints of life. If you direct your attention to outer conditions and circumstances, which are constantly changing, you are bound to limit yourself and inhibit your prosperity. Direct your attention to God and let the wisdom and power of God come first in your life and then your eye will be single and all your undertakings will be blessed.

Six in the third place: *Thou wilt shew me the path of life . . .* (Psalms 16:11). Claim and know that Infinite Intelligence within your subconscious mind reveals to you the next step in your unfoldment, and follow the *lead* which comes clearly into your conscious, reasoning mind. Divine right action governs you at all times.

Six in the fourth place: . . . *the kingdom of Heaven is at hand* (Matthew 3:2). The Kingdom of Infinite Intelligence, Boundless Wisdom and all the powers of the God-head are within you. Knowing that, become a King over your own conceptive realm. Think right, feel right, act right, be right and do right. You have absolute control over your thoughts, imagery, emotions, actions and reactions. Conform to the Divine law of harmony in all ways. Exercise your prerogatives as a King over your mind.

Nine in the fifth place: *The way of life is above to the wise . . .* (Proverbs 15:24). You are here to express more and more of life, love, truth and beauty. Your motivation for others is to bless and prosper them in all ways.

Nine in the sixth place: *Blessed are the pure in heart, for they shall see God* (Matthew 5:8). "Purity" in Biblical language means that you contemplate and recognize God alone as the only real Cause and the only real Power. As you dwell on God's love and harmony in your life, you discover and experience escape from all sickness and trouble, and you are able to impart wisdom and goodwill to others.

## 21. Shih Ho/Biting Through

——<br>
— — **above Li, The Clinging, Fire**<br>
——<br>
— —<br>
— — **below Chen, The Arousing, Thunder**<br>
——

*The Judgment*

*This book of the law shall not depart out of thy mouth . . . for then thou shalt make thy way prosperous, and then thou shalt have good success* (Joshua 1:8). As you contemplate your good, know that the Almighty Power is backing you up and that all obstructions will be overcome. Know that everything is working out in Divine order for you.

*The Image*

*Thus saith the Lord God . . . remove violence and spoil, and execute judgment and justice . . .* (Ezekiel 45:9). Every action of yours must be based on right action and justice. Do not compromise with that which is right. The judgment or decision in your mind must be based on the universal law of harmony and goodwill to all.

*The Lines*

Nine at the bottom: *If thy foot offend thee, cut it off . . .* (Mark 9:45). The word "foot" in the Bible means understanding. What is your understanding of life? You must stand on the laws of life which never change. You must stand on the eternal principle of harmony, love, right action and peace. You must never deviate from the truth.

Cut yourself off mentally from ulterior motives, and also permit no one else to take advantage of you.

Six in the second place: . . . *noses have they, but they smell not* (Psalms 115:6). To smell in the symbolism of the Bible is to practice discernment, i.e., you separate the wheat from the chaff, the good from the evil, and adhere to that which is lovely and of good report. Stand firm for that which you know to be right and good.

Six in the third place: . . . *my meat is to do the will of him that sent me* . . . (John 4:34). The word "meat" in the Bible means the qualities, powers and attributes of God. Meditate on courage, faith, confidence, joy, love and goodwill—this is the meat of Heaven. If you chew on ill will, bitterness, hostility and anger, you should be aware that these emotions are poisonous and tend to debilitate your entire organism. Keep away from all mental poisons and exalt God in the midst of you.

Nine in the fourth place: . . . *I have meat to eat that ye know not of* (John 4:32). There is an Invisible Power and Presence always available to you. Be firm and persevere. Realize and know that an Almighty Power is backing you up. You will be inspired and guided in all ways, and experience fulfillment of your heart's desire.

Six in the fifth place: *But strong meat belongeth to them that are of full age, even those who by reason of use have their senses exercised to discern both good and evil* (Hebrews 5:14). It is necessary for you to assume the role of emotional and spiritual maturity. Never yield to that which is false. Be faithful to the truth, while realizing that what's right action for you is right action for everyone.

Nine in the sixth place: *And they shall turn away their ears from the truth* . . . (II Timothy 4:4). Any time you refuse to listen to the Truth of Being and insist on having your own way, you will get into trouble and experience loss and failure.

22. Pi/Grace

——

— — **above Ken, Keeping Still, Mountain**

— —

——

— — **below Li, The Clinging, Fire**

——

*The Judgment*

*For by grace are ye saved through faith . . .* (Ephesians 2:8). Grace is the mathematical and accurate response of the Infinite Intelligence to your habitual thinking and imagining. As you call upon Infinite Intelligence, the response is inevitable and coincides with the nature of your request. You will succeed in your pursuits under the guidance of God.

*The Image*

*Let us therefore come boldly unto the throne of grace . . . and find grace to help in time of need* (Hebrews 4:16). Turn to the Indwelling God for guidance and inspiration, and your decisions will be right for all concerned.

*The Lines*

Nine at the bottom: *Grace be to you and peace from God . . .* (II Corinthians 1:2). Grace means that state wherein the Spirit of God is operating in you to regenerate and strengthen you. Follow the Divine path, and Divine love will go before you, making straight and joyous your way.

Six in the second place: *Let your speech be always with grace, seasoned with salt, that ye may know how ye ought to answer every man* (Colossians 4:6). This means that your thoughts, words and actions should conform to the Golden Rule and the law of love. You have salt in your speech when you speak the truth with zeal and enthusiasm. Salt adds flavor to food and makes it more palatable; likewise, when your words encourage, enthuse and enlighten others you are lending color to whatever you say or do.

Nine in the third place: *Looking diligently lest any man fail of the grace of God . . .* (Hebrews 12:15). Be diligent and watchful. Let the Spirit of God govern and guide you and continue moving forward, and assured victory will be yours.

Six in the fourth place: *. . . we have access by faith into this grace . . .* (Romans 5:2). Your faith is in the goodness of God, in the power of God and in all things good. The God-Presence in you responds to your desire, and the fulfillment of your plans takes place.

Six in the fifth place: *Thus saith the Lord, the people . . . found grace in the wilderness . . .* (Jeremiah 31:2). Wherever you are, you can stir up the gift of God within you and feel His Presence governing and directing you. There is no great or small in the God that made us all. Love in your heart will find love and felicity everywhere. Love conquers all. Great success is assured you.

Nine in the sixth place: *. . . the Lord will give grace and glory; no good thing will be withheld from them that walk uprightly* (Psalms 84:11). God is now flowing through you, filling up all the empty vessels in your life. Divine love flows through your thoughts, words and deeds. All good is yours.

## 23. Po/Splitting Apart

———

— — **above Ken, Keeping Still, Mountain**

— —

— —

— — **below K'un, The Receptive, Earth**

— —

### *The Judgment*

. . . *and a house divided against a house falleth* (Luke 11:17). The house is your mind, and when there is conflict in your mind it is unwise to undertake any new venture. Remain still and quiet, contemplate the peace of God and the harmony of God in your mind, body and worldly circumstances; and gradually you will get into a balanced state of mind. Place your trust in God's guidance.

### *The Image*

. . . *whosoever shall say unto this mountain, Be thou removed, and be thou cast into the sea; and shall not doubt in his heart, but shall believe that those things which he saith shall come to pass; he shall have whatsoever he saith* (Mark 11:23). If there be a mountain of fear, remorse, debt, or hurtful habits or ill health, realize every problem is Divinely outmatched. As you grapple with it courageously with faith and confidence in the Omnipotence of God, you will overcome the mountain (obstacle) and it will disappear and be cast into oblivion. You will experience a Divine solution.

### *The Lines*

Six at the bottom: . . . *take up thy bed and walk* (Mark 2:9). It is wrong to cohabit with negative thoughts and imagery in the bed of your mind, as you will bring forth negative experiences and conditions. Remain still and quiet and realize that nothing is forever, and everything passes away. Fill your mind with the truths of God and keep on affirming, "God loves me and cares for me." Divest yourself at once of all negative and destructive thoughts, as these would bring on loss and failure.

Six in the second place: . . . *I have made my bed in the darkness* (Job 17:13). The people who inhabit your mind are thoughts, beliefs, opinions and images. Darkness is an absence of light, and a bed means that what you are lying down with in your mind, i.e., what you are cohabiting with, being negative, will spawn negative results. The Bible tells you that the enemies are of your own household (mind). Read the 91st and the 23rd Psalms and realize one with God is a majority. Remember the old aphoristic statement: "This, too, shall pass away."

Six in the third place: *Thou wilt keep him in perfect peace whose mind is stayed on thee* . . . (Isaiah 26:3). Keep your mind stayed upon the Indwelling God and His love. Claim: "God is guiding me now. Divine peace fills my soul. My faith is in God and all things good, and all the negation of my mind is destroyed by the healing light of God's love saturating my subconscious mind."

Six in the fourth place: . . . *forasmuch as he defiled his father's bed, his birthright was given* . . . (I Chronicles 5:1). To defile his father's bed means to pollute your mind with anger, self-condemnation, resentment, and the like. These are mental poisons which bring forth lack and limitation in all phases of your life. The thing to do is to forgive yourself for harboring negative thoughts, wish for everyone all the blessings of life, and exalt God in the midst of you, mighty to heal all conditions.

Six in the fifth place: *And he saith unto them, Follow me, and I will make you fishers of men* (Matthew 4:19). The word "man" means mind, and you can fish the idea out of the depths of your mind. You can't follow any man, but you can identify with the eternal verities and the laws of your mind. These you can apply and follow. You can fish out of your subconscious mind the solution to any problem. The answer is within. Divine answers and ideas are welling up from your subconscious depths, and everything you do will prosper. The answer comes to you now.

Nine at the top: *But the fruit of the Spirit is love, joy, peace, long-*

*suffering, gentleness, goodness, faith, meekness, temperance: against such there is no law* (Galatians 5:22, 23). When we eat of the Tree of Life (Presence of God) within us, i.e., when we medidate on harmony, peace, love, joy and inspiration, we are absorbing these truths so that they become automatically expressed in our lives in the same way as a piece of bread is transmuted into flesh and blood. As you incorporate the truths of God in your subconscious mind, you will suddenly discover all sorts of wonders happening in your life. Remember, all evil ultimately destroys itself. The mills of the gods grind slowly, but they grind exceedingly fine. Your faith and confidence in the good will be amply rewarded here and now.

## 24. Fu/Return (The Turning Point)

— —
— — **above K'un, The Receptive, Earth**
— —
— —
— — **below Chen, The Arousing, Thunder**
——

*The Judgment*

*. . . in returning and rest shall ye be saved; in quietness and in confidence shall be your strength . . .* (Isaiah 30:15). *If thou return to the Almighty, thou shalt be built up . . .* (Job 22:23). This means, as you align yourself with the Infinite Presence within you, this Power becomes active and potent in your life. In this inner communion with the Divine, you feel the strength, guidance and love of His Presence. Under this spiritual influence, it is to your advantage to undertake a new venture, and whatever you decide on will prosper.

*The Image*

*The voice of thy thunder was in the heaven: the lightnings lightened the world* . . . (Psalms 77:18). This means the heavens of your own mind, where you feel the inspiration of the Infinite and you are stirred up and lifted up spiritually. The lightning refers to the inner light or illumination of your intellect by the wisdom of God. This is an excellent time for you to become still and quiet and listen, as Emerson said, "to the whisperings of the gods."

*The Lines*

Nine at the bottom: . . . *and my prayer returned into mine own bosom* (Psalms 35:13). As a routine procedure, make a habit of supplanting every negative thought with a constructive one. Focus your attention on your goal or ideal, nourish it and sustain it mentally and emotionally, and it will sink into your subconscious mind. Great success and happiness are yours now.

Six in the second place: *And shalt return unto the Lord thy God and shalt obey his voice* . . . (Deuteronomy 30:2). It is God in action in your life, which means all around harmony and peace. Listen to your inner voice of intuition, and it will lead you to green pastures and abundance in all things.

Six in the third place: . . . *and cut off from it him that passeth out and him that returneth* (Ezekiel 35:7). When you procrastinate, vacillate, waver and for some reason can't make up your mind, you are like the double-minded man, unstable in all his ways. Cling to the truth and busy your mind with ideas which heal, bless, inspire, elevate and dignify your soul. Refuse to deviate from the spiritual standard of whatsoever is lovely, noble and God-like.

Six in the fourth place: *And the shepherds returned, glorifying and praising God* . . . (Luke 2:20). Your mind needs a shepherd. Continue to watch over your thoughts, attitudes and feelings and walk in the consciousness of God's love, and you will automatically express as well as experience good fortune.

Six in the fifth place: . . . *Return unto me and I will return unto you, saith the Lord of hosts* . . . (Malachi 3:7). Whenever you turn to the God-Presence within you, there is an automatic response. It is the law of reciprocal relationship. The God-Power never punishes. Instead, you punish yourself by negative thinking, and you heal yourself by constructive thinking. Reward and retribution are based solely on your thinking and acting. Forgive yourself for harboring negative thoughts and resolve not to indulge yourself in this manner any more, and you are forgiven and free.

Six at the top: *And I said after she had done all these things, Turn thou unto me, but she returned not . . .* (Jeremiah 3:7). Whatever errors you may have committed, you can begin now to give constructive, life-giving, spiritual patterns to your subconscious mind, and there will be an immediate and automatic response of your deeper mind in conformity with your new standards. There is no time or space as such in mind, and the minute you begin to use the law righteously, the past is forgotten and remembered no more. If you refuse to redirect your life along God-like ways, you will experience losses, failures and obstacles along all lines.

## 25. Wu Wang/Innocence (The Unexpected)

——

—— **above Ch'ien, The Creative, Heaven**

——

— —

— — **below Chen, The Arousing, Thunder**

——

*The Judgment*

*I am clean without transgression, I am innocent; neither is there iniquity in me* (Job 33:9). To be innocent means to be without sin, to be free from moral wrong, guiltless. To be innocent also implies a complete lack of evil intent or motive. This is a universe of law and order, and in this universe nothing happens by chance. Good luck and bad luck do not enter the situation. When your *motivation* is right and you claim that Divine law and order are governing you, you will move forward successfully to your goal.

*The Image*

*. . . and I heard, as it were the noise of thunder . . .* (Revelation 6:1). The "lightnings" and "thunderings" mentioned in the *I Ching* and in the Bible mean the movement of consciousness from the unconditioned to the conditioned state. It means a quickening of the Spirit of God in you moving you forward in life's journey.

*The Lines*

Nine at the bottom: *My God hath sent his angel, and hath shut the lions' mouths, that they have not hurt me; forasmuch as before him innocence was found in me . . .* (Daniel 6:22). The "angel" represents the inner urges, the ideas welling up within you telling you to rise up ever higher. The lions represent obstacles, problems and difficulties. All these will be overcome and success and happiness are assured.

Six in the second place: *. . . he hath set an harvest for thee . . .* (Hosea 6:11). Whatever you sow in your subconscious mind will come forth as form, conditions and events. That is the harvest you reap. Your subconscious reproduces your habitual thinking. Your subconscious multiplies and magnifies what you deposit. Is it good or bad? Don't wonder how, when or where your prayer will be answered; but trust the deeper mind to bring it to pass in its own way.

Six in the third place: *. . . for I have found the piece which I had lost* (Luke 15:9). When you lose your contact with God and when you fail to keep prayed up, loss comes into your experience in various ways. If you have experienced loss, you can go into the realm of your mind and there identify with your good, knowing that your subconscious mind will respond and further multiply your good. Refuse to accept the loss in your mind, as all transactions such as gain and loss take place in your mind. Mentally and spiritually unite with that which you say you have lost, and your subconscious will replenish your possessions in ways you know not of. You can't lose what belongs to you by right of consciousness.

Nine in the fourth place: *Praying always with all prayer . . . and watching thereunto with all perseverance . . .* (Ephesians 6:18). Your determination and right attitude enable you to reach your goal. Nothing and no one can oppose the Power of the Infinite moving on your behalf.

Nine in the fifth place: *A merry heart doeth good like a medicine . . .* (Proverbs 17:22). Realize that the Infinite Healing Presence Which created you is now flowing through you as harmony, health and peace. The tendency of the Life Principle is to heal and to restore you to perfect health. When you consult a doctor, realize that he is God's man and that God is guiding him, and that whatever he suggests you do can only bless you. Perfect health is assured you.

Nine in the sixth place: *To everything there is a season, and a time to every purpose under the heaven* (Ecclesiastes 3:1). God is timeless and spaceless, but you are living objectively in a three-dimensional time and space world. There is a right time to sow and a right time to reap. Remain quiet and still; bide your time. The right time to advance will come later.

## 26. Ta Ch'u/The Taming Power of the Great

———
— — **above Ken, Keeping Still, Mountain**
— —
———
——— **below Ch'ien, The Creative, Heaven**
———

*The Judgment*

. . . *But he that endureth to the end shall be saved* (Matthew 10:22). This means that as you stick to your goal, full of confidence and faith in the Almighty Power to back you up, you will succeed. It is to your advantage to intend your mind vigorously and decisively in a new direction. This means that you travel mentally from where you are to a new location in your mind, and that having made the decision, an external journey would also be a blessing.

*The Image*

. . . *behold, the Kingdom of God is within you* (Luke 17:21). All the powers, qualities and attributes of God are within you. The treasures of eternity are within you. Contemplate harmony, health, peace, love, right action and Divine guidance. Live with these truths and wonders will happen in your life.

*The Lines*

Nine at the bottom: . . . *and when sailing was now dangerous* . . . (Acts 27:9). There is a time when it is right to hug the shore, rather than to adventure out on the sea in the presence of a storm. Sit steady in the boat (remain poised and calm) and the time will come for you to move forward in Divine order.

Nine in the second place: . . . *and the axletrees of the wheels were joined to the base* . . . (I Kings 7:32). As you well know, the axle is the bar around which a wheel rotates. When you join up mentally and spiritually with God, right action follows. In the symbology of the *I Ching* and the Bible, when axletrees are removed, no motion is possible. This points out to you that you should still your mind, attend to routine matters and know that you will be guided in personal advancement at the right time and in the right way.

Nine in the third place: *And I saw, and behold a white horse: and he that sat on him had a bow; and a crown was given unto him: and he went forth conquering, and to conquer* (Revelation 6:2). You ride the white horse (the Power of the Presence of God) when you realize that your own awareness, I AMness, is the only cause, substance and power. When you trust the God-Presence completely, when you give all your allegiance and devotion to the sovereignty and supremacy of the One Power, you are truly riding the white horse to victory. Refuse to give power to conditions, circumstances and events. Everything you meet is Divinely outmatched, and you will reach your goal and accomplish your aim in life.

Six in the fourth place: *Not by might, nor by power, but by my spirit, saith the Lord . . .* (Zechariah 4:6). Effortless effort is the answer. You can't add power to the Infinite Power which is the only power in the universe. Let this power flow through you easily, quietly and lovingly, knowing that the Spirit in you is bringing all things to pass in Divine order. Use no mental coercion or force. Easy does it. You will conquer.

Six in the fifth place: *The boar out of the wood doth waste it . . .* (Psalms 80:13). The animal propensities within us must be checked. Animals in the *I Ching* and in our Bible represent animated states of consciousness, such as emotions, feelings, tones, moods and vibrations. Your emotional nature must be channeled constructively. Remain peaceful and confident, and you will achieve your heart's desire.

Nine in the sixth place: *. . . the Lord's throne is in heaven . . .* (Psalms 11:4). Heaven is your mind at peace; the Lord's throne is the Lordly Power or the God-Presence in you—the Reality of you. The Living Spirit (God) within you is now moving through you, bringing the blessings of life to you and the fulfillment of your desires.

## 27. I/The Corners of the Mouth (Providing Nourishment)

———
— —  **above Ken, Keeping Still, Mountain**
— —
— —
— —  **below Chen, The Arousing, Thunder**
———

*The Judgment*

*For the Lord giveth wisdom; out of his mouth cometh knowledge and understanding* (Proverbs 2:6). The mouth of God is the mind of man. Your mind should be fed with wisdom, truth and beauty, faith and confidence, and inspiration from On High. This is the right food for your mind. Fill your mind with the truths of God and you will crowd out of your mind everything unlike God. Be critical and selective of what enters your mind, and make sure it is wholesome and true. As you continue dwelling mentally on the truths of God, you will experience great blessings.

*The Image*

*. . . but the thunder of his power who can understand?* (Job 26:14). "Thunder" in the *I Ching* and in our Bible means the quickening of the Spirit in you, i.e., you begin to think, speak and act from the standpoint of the Infinite One, and your speech and expressions are based on wisdom, truth and love. Whatever you say to others should help, encourage and inspire them.

*The Lines*

Nine at the bottom: *These also shall be unclean unto you among the creeping things . . . and the tortoise after his kind* (Leviticus

11:29). The tortoise is slow moving and crawls along the earth. This represents a worm-of-the-dust attitude—indicative of one who looks at appearances and the surface of things only. You have the capacity to go to the Fountain of Life within you and there claim what you want: riches, success, eminence in your profession; and the Life Principle will respond to your claim. You can get from the Infinite whatever you need without hurting the hair of a living being and without impinging on the rights and freedom of others in any way. Emerson said, "Envy is ignorance and imitation is suicide." To be envious of others denotes inferiority and inadequacy, and this attitude attracts more loss, lack and limitation to you.

Six in the second place: . . . *nourished up in the words of faith and of good doctrine, whereunto thou hast attained* (I Timothy 4:6). Seek guidance, strength and inspiration from the God-Presence within you. The Infinite Intelligence of your subconscious will guide you to your true place in life. It is wrong to lean on others and to look to them for support. Life's primary lesson is to prepare you to stand on your own feet and overcome your problems. The man who leans on others and accepts help too easily is destroying his self-esteem, self-reliance and character development. This attitude is one of failure.

Six in the third place: *And there will I nourish thee . . . lest thou . . . come to poverty* (Genesis 45:11). You cannot live by bread alone in this world. You need invisible food such as courage, faith, confidence, joy, laughter and inspiration from God. The mass mind with its fears, anxieties, worries, envies, jealousies and negative propaganda is not the proper food, as it leads to loss, sickness and confusion. It is never too late to turn back to the One, the Beautiful and the Good.

Six in the fourth place: *I will nourish you and your little ones. And he comforted them and spake kindly unto them* (Genesis 50:21). You must keep on the alert and feed your mind the ideal food and defend and protect your mind from fear, doubt and negativity of all kinds. Force your attention on the good and remember that the mighty Power of God can bring your dreams to pass. Inner perception will enable you to attract to yourself the ideal helpers on the way.

Six in the fifth place: . . . *and ye shall find rest unto your souls*

(Matthew 11:29). Turn to the God-Presence within you and claim His river of peace, power and strength are flowing through you, guiding and directing you. It would be good for you to see a wise man in your area and get spiritual and mental help. In the meantime, remain quiet and still and avoid journeys. The right time will come.

Nine at the top: . . . *he feedeth among the lilies until the day breaks and the shadows flee away* . . . (Song of Solomon 2:16–17). Feed among the lilies of God and Heaven, such as joy, harmony, peace, beauty and Divine law and order. All your plans, journeys and undertakings will prosper. Continue in this abiding trust and faith in God until the day breaks and the shadows flee away.

## 28. Ta Kuo/Preponderance of the Great

— —
——— **above Tui, The Joyous, Lake**
———
———
——— **below Sun, The Gentle, Wind, Wood**
— —

*The Judgment*

*Cast thy burden upon the Lord and he shall sustain thee* . . . (Psalms 55:22). When you feel the load or burden too great, remember there is a God-Power within you that can sustain you, strengthen you and solve your problems. It is a change in feeling and conviction that matters. Since it is prayer which lifts you up, an effective affirmation follows: "I am surrounded, supported and guided by the love, wisdom and peace of God." You will succeed and reach your goal in life.

*The Image*

*God is in the midst of her; she shall not be moved: God shall help her, and that right early* (Psalms 46:5). "Waters" in the Bible means emotions. Do not be disturbed. God is really in the midst of you, calming the waters. Realize that God's river of peace flows through you, then you shall not be moved, but shall remain serene and calm.

*The Lines*

Six at the bottom: . . . *be courteous* (I Peter 3:8). Politeness and courtesy mean that you do and say the kindest thing in the kindest way. Kindness is a child of love. Be ever watchful that you conduct yourself according to the great law of love and kindness.

Nine in the second place: *We hanged our harps upon the willows* . . . (Psalms 137:2). This means you are stirring up the gift of God within you. The harp symbolizes music of the soul or an inner joy which causes you to rise above all limitations and to accomplish great things, and you will be blessed by whatever you do.

Nine in the third place: . . . *when sailing was now dangerous* . . . (Acts 27:9). When there is a storm at sea, it is best not to venture forth in your boat. Seek guidance and counsel. Remain calm. Mental coercion and trying to force things lead to loss and failure.

Nine in the fourth place: *Put on therefore . . . humbleness of mind* . . . (Colossians 3:12). *Before honor is humility* (Proverbs 15:33). It is of great importance to possess humility. Be receptive and teachable, and growth and achievement will follow. The great ones of the earth are humble and honest, and their motivations are good. Trust the God-Power to give you strength, power and guidance, and your success is assured.

Nine in the fifth place: *They shall still bring forth fruit in old age* . . . (Psalms 92:14). Youth is a time for all sorts of games and participation in many types of athletics. As you grow in years, you should become intensely interested in mental and spiritual truths. Don't try to recapture so-called "lost youth." Your job now is to release the great truths of God within you. If you are sixty-five or seventy, you can't run as fast as your son of nineteen. Don't try it; if you do, you are *as a bird that hasteth to the snare and knoweth not that it is for his life* (Proverbs 7:23).

Six in the sixth place: . . . *being overflowed with water, perished* (II Peter 3:6). A flood of negativity in the mind can bring on edema and inner accumulation of fluids which could have very negative results. Calm the waters of your mind and realize that God in the midst of you can bring you peace, harmony and freedom.

## 29. K'an/The Abysmal (Water)

— —
—— **above K'an, The Abysmal, Water**
— —
— —
—— **below K'an, The Abysmal, Wate**
— —

*The Judgment*

*Though the waters thereof roar and be troubled* . . . (Psalms 46:3). You are no longer drifting and being tossed about by every wind that blows, nor are you being swept along like a piece of driftwood at the mercy of the waves. Your trust is in God to lead you to green pastures and still waters.

*The Image*

*When thou passest through the waters, I will be with thee, and through the rivers they shall not overflow thee* . . . (Isaiah 43:2).

Realize and know that Divine love goes before you making straight and joyous your ways. God flows through you, filling up all the empty vessels of your life.

*The Lines*

Six at the bottom: *I have gone astray like a lost sheep* . . . (Psalms 119:176). When you deviate from the Divine standard of whatsoever things are true, lovely, noble and God-like, you experience loss and limitation. Get back on the beam of God's glory and let God's love and right action govern all your actions.

Nine in the second place: *The steps of a good man are ordered by the Lord: and he delighteth in his way* (Psalms 37:23). Do not force things now. Do not permit any mental resistance. Turn to the Indwelling God and claim that all your steps are Divinely ordered. Be alert, on the *qui vive*, and use basic common sense, which is extremely uncommon.

Six in the third place: *In my distress, I cried unto the Lord, and he heard me* (Psalms 120:1). When you are in a quandary and don't know which way to turn, quiet your mind and ask Infinite Intelligence to reveal the way out to you. The answer will come. Heed it. There is always an answer and a solution.

Six in the fourth place: *Unto the upright there ariseth light in the darkness* . . . (Psalms 112:4). God in you, the Inner Light, is an inner dynamic Power. It will be your light and will enable you to do and say the right thing at the right time to all those around you.

Nine in the fifth place: *He that is greedy of gain troubleth his own house* . . . (Proverbs 15:27). Let there be no strife or contention in your mind. Do not try to reach too far or grant more than you are mentally ready to receive. Trust the Creative Intelligence of your subconscious to lead and guide you to safety, and It will do precisely that.

Six in the sixth place: . . . *but went and cast him into prison, till he should pay the debt* (Matthew 18:30). There is the prison of fear, sickness, resentment and ill will which keeps man in bondage and thralldom. Stone walls do not a prison make nor iron bars a cage. The greatest prison is the prison of the mind where guilt followed by self-punishment creates havoc with men. Forgive yourself for harboring negative thoughts, and be sure you forgive everybody else. You know when you have succeeded in forgiving others, because you no longer sizzle mentally when you think of them. Come out of your mental prison and let in the sunshine of God's love.

## 30. Li/The Clinging, Fire

———
— — **above Li, The Clinging, Fire**
———
———
— — **below Li, The Clinging, Fire**
———

*The Judgment*

*. . . but he that endureth to the end shall be saved* (Matthew 10:22). This means you should persist in your goal with faith and confidence, knowing that the wisdom of your subconscious will sustain you and guide you. Guard your conscious mind and see to it that nothing enters into your subconscious mind* that does not fill your soul with joy and freedom.

*The Image*

*And the light of Israel shall be for a fire . . .* (Isaiah 10:17). Fire in the Bible and *I Ching* means illumination, or the Supreme Intelligence of your subconscious mind, revealing to you everything you need to know and enabling you to direct that light on others.

*See *The Power of Your Subconscious Mind*, by Joseph Murphy (Englewood Cliffs, N.J.: Prentice-Hall, Inc., 1963).

*The Lines*

Nine at the bottom: *Thou wilt keep him in perfect peace whose mind is stayed on thee* . . . (Isaiah 26:3). Be sure that you are not governed and impressed with the fears, doubts, apprehensions and propaganda of the world. The first thing in the morning, tune in with the Infinite and claim Divine guidance, Divine law and order and inspiration from On High. Charge your mental and spiritual batteries with confidence in God and all things good. The beginning and the end are the same. Begin with God and the outcome will be good.

Six in the second place: *And he shall bring forth thy righteousness as the light, and thy judgment as the noonday* (Psalms 37:6). At noon the sun casts no shadow. Nothing can deflect you from your aim as you are Divinely led by your inner guiding principle to a triumphant success.

Nine in the third place: . . . *when the sun did set, they brought unto him all that were diseased* . . . (Mark 1:32). The sun in the Bible and in the *I Ching* represents the Infinite Life Principle, or the Infinite Intelligence, which gives life to all men—symbolic of the sun, which gives light and life to the world. You live forever, as life cannot die. When you refuse to turn to the Healing Light within you, which can heal, bless and inspire you, the sun has set, for you, because you are accepting the false beliefs and opinions of the world. This attitude brings loss to you. Old age is not the flight of years but the dawn of wisdom in the mind of men.

Nine in the fourth place: . . . *the flaming flame shall not be quenched* . . . (Ezekiel 20:47). . . . *in thy light shall we see light* (Psalms 36:9). The Eternal Light is within you. It will keep shining for you all the time if you tune in on the Infinite, realizing that you can do all things by means of the God-Power within you. Everything you do should be according to Divine law and order. Give up the belief that your strength comes from your brain, nerves or muscles. Your strength and success come from God within you. Avoid the ups and downs and the great swings of fortune by doing all things for the glory of God. To strive, maneuver and jockey yourself into a high position without having the mental equivalent is vain, because the law of your mind will cause you to lose it. Stop trying to promote yourself externally—you promote yourself when you have succeeded in impregnating your subconscious with the idea of growth, expansion, success and right action.

Six in the fifth place: *And God shall wipe away all tears from their eyes . . .* (Revelation 21:4). Nothing is forever. Grief, sorrow, sickness all pass away. Joy displaces sadness, tears give way to gladness. After the storm comes the calm. When depressed or sad, focus your attention on the solution, the way out, and all the powers of the God-head will flow to that focal point of attention, and you will thus experience the joy of the answered prayer.

Nine in the sixth place: *Be not overcome of evil, but overcome evil with good* (Romans 12:21). The word "live," when spelled backward, is "evil." This means you are going against the stream of Life, which moves harmoniously, peacefully and lovingly, for God is Life. You can cremate, burn up, all the negative thoughts in your own mind by supplanting them with thoughts of harmony, peace, love and goodwill to all. Ideas of resentment, vengeance, ill will and hostility are gangsters in your mind. They are usurpers and marauders. Banish them from your mind and, instead, contemplate beauty, Divine order and peace. You are a king over your conceptive realm, and you are an absolute monarch over your thoughts, feelings, emotions, actions and reactions. Assume your sovereignty now.

## 31. Hsien/Influence (Wooing)

— —<br>
——— **above Tui, The Joyous, Lake**<br>
———<br>
———<br>
— — **below Ken, Keeping Still, Mountain**<br>
— —

*The Judgment*

*This book of the law shall not depart out of thy mouth . . . for then thou shalt make thy way prosperous, and then thou shalt have good success* (Joshua 1:8). The law of mind is that whenever you impregnate an idea or desire in your subconscious mind, the latter brings it to pass. Practice stick-to-itiveness and determination by nourishing mentally and emotionally your ideal, and all will be well. Marriage in the Bible and in the *I Ching* means a mental and spiritual union with your good. It may also mean a marital union between a man and woman who harmonize with each other.

*The Image*

*. . . he stood by the lake of Gennesaret* (Luke 5:1). The lake in the Bible and in the *I Ching* means the sea of Divine Life where all the treasures of the Infinite abide. In everyday language, the lake is your own subconscious mind. Look for guidance and direction from the Infinite Intelligence within your subconscious mind. Be humble and receptive to the inner wisdom which transcends your intellect. It is that which knows all and sees all.

*The Lines*

Six at the bottom: *And as the toes of the feet were part of iron, and part of clay, so the kingdom shall be partly strong, and partly broken* (Daniel 2:42). "Feet" means understanding, comprehension of Divine laws. The "toe" indicates your thought or ideal, your plan or purpose; and if it is not backed up by feeling and enthusiasm, it will not be objectified. "Iron" symbolizes strength, stability and power; "clay" means the objective world; and if you think that conditions, circumstances and people can thwart your plan, you are giving power to created things and not to the Creator, thereby blocking your good.

Six in the second place: *Every place that the sole of your foot shall tread upon, that have I given unto you . . .* (Joshua 1:3). This means that except you enter into a fixed and definite psychological state and are motivated by Divine right action, you should not go forward with your plans. "Foot" in the *I Ching* and in the Bible means understanding.

Nine in the third place: . . . *he touched the hollow of his thigh* . . . (Genesis 32:25). The thigh is a euphemistic expression meaning the phallic organs of man, which are symbolic of the creative powers that constitute your conscious and subconscious mind. When your conscious and subconscious agree on that which is lovely and of good report, you are using your creative power constructively. If you are conditioned by negative emotions or by ulterior motives and wish to take advantage of others, the results will be very negative for you.

Nine in the fourth place: *Casting all your cares upon him, for he careth for you* (I Peter 5:7). The kingdom of heaven is within you, and its atmosphere is peace, harmony, joy, love and beauty. Quiet your mind, submit yourself to Divine guidance and Divine love, and you will succeed. Cling steadfastly to the truth that there is within you an answer to every prayer, peace for discord and abundant supply for every need. Never under any circumstances try to coerce the minds of others or take advantage of them in any way. Such an attitude ultimately leads to loss and confusion.

Nine in the fifth place: *In his neck remaineth strength, and sorrow is turned into joy before him* (Job 41:22). Your neck is on a pivot, and symbolically it means that you can always turn to the truth about any situation and be governed by the mood of harmony, right action and goodwill. Feel the Spirit of the Almighty governing and directing you in all ways. Such an attitude always brings good results.

Six in the sixth place: *The tongue of the wise useth knowledge aright: but the mouth of fools poureth out foolishness* (Proverbs 15:2). *A wholesome tongue is a tree of life: but perverseness therein is a breach in the spirit* (Proverbs 15:4). Your speech must be based on the values of life and on the eternal verities. You should think and speak from the standpoint of the Infinite. Idle chatter and mere verbalisms accomplish nothing. Sincerity and honesty are felt subconsciously by others; what you say should come from your heart and should be based on love and goodwill.

## 32. HENG/DURATION

— —
— — **above Chen, The Arousing, Thunder**
———
———
——— **below Sun, The Gentle, Wind**
— —

*The Judgment*

*Riches and honour are with me; yea, durable riches and righteousness* (Proverbs 8:18). As you continue steadfastly in right thought, right feeling and right action, you will experience riches of the mind, such as harmony, health and peace, and also an abundance of all the material riches you need. Whatever you plan to achieve and whatever destination you plan to reach will be successful.

*The Image*

*. . . I heard, as it were the noise of thunder . . .* (Revelation 6:1). *And a man shall be as an hiding place from the wind . . .* (Isaiah 32:2). One of the meanings of thunder is the noise of the world or the winds of fear and anxiety. You remain unmoved, because you are governed by an immutable law—the same yesterday, today and forever. You are governed by an Infinite Guiding Principle, and Divine law and order govern you and lead you to your goal.

*The Lines*

Six at the bottom: *Go not forth hastily to strive lest thou know not what to do in the end thereof . . .* (Proverbs 25:8). Realize that in quietness and in confidence lies your strength. It is the quiet, composed, peaceful mind that gets things done. You can't force a child's growth. The child will develop and grow according to a Universal Law. Thoughtless, rash or undue speech leads to failure. Haste makes waste.

Nine in the second place: *Remember ye not the former things, neither consider the things of old* (Isaiah 43:18). The past is dead. Have no regret over past actions. A new beginning is a new end. The law of your mind, like the laws of chemistry, mathematics or physics, has no grudge against you. The minute you begin to think right, feel right and act right, there is an immediate and automatic response of your subconscious mind which brings your good to pass.

Nine in the third place: *A double minded man is unstable in all his ways* (James 1:8). A vacillating, wavering neurotic state of mind leads to confusion and failure. Your inner state of mind determines all your experiences in life, and if you permit the avalanche of fears, doubts, anxieties and propaganda of the world to govern you, the result is lack and limitation. Your subconscious assumptions, beliefs and convictions dictate and control all your conscious actions. Think right and your actions will be right.

Nine in the fourth place: *The Lord is my shepherd, I shall not want* (Psalms 23:1). The "Lord" means the Supreme Intelligence within you that knows all and sees all. This Infinite Intelligence is none other than your Higher Self, and if you choose It to watch over you and guide you as a shepherd watches over his sheep, you will be Divinely led in all your ways. Affirm: "Infinite Intelligence leads me to my true place in life where I am doing what I love to do, Divinely happy and Divinely prospered," and follow the *lead* which comes to you. There is no occasion to be misplaced or maladjusted in life or to be a square peg in a round hole.

Six in the fifth place: *For the husband is the head of the wife . . .* (Ephesians 5:23). The wife in the Bible and the *I Ching* means your emotional nature, or the subconscious. The husband is your thought, idea, or the conscious, reasoning mind. Your subconscious is controlled by your conscious mind. Emotion follows thought, and if you want to control your emotions, you must first control your habitual thinking. Let your conscious mind be aware and accept the fact that Infinite Intelligence guides and directs you, and the woman (your subconscious) will respond. You should not let negative emotions govern your judgments or decisions. Reason things out in your mind and then choose the good, the true, and the God-like decision, and your emotion will back you up.

Six in the sixth place: . . . *in quietness and in confidence shall be your strength* . . . (Isaiah 30:15). When your conscious mind is serene, calm and tranquil, the wisdom of the subconscious rises to the surface mind and reveals answers to you. If you are not in tune with the Infinite and permit yourself, instead, to be controlled and governed by fear, anxiety and the false beliefs of the mass mind, confusion and failure follow. Remember, it is a quiet mind that gets things done.

## 33. TUN/RETREAT

———
——— **above Ch'ien, The Creative, Heaven**
———
———
— — **below Ken, Keeping Still, Mountain**
— —

*The Judgment*

. . . *In returning and rest shall ye be saved* . . . (Isaiah 30:15). Return to the Infinite within you and mentally claim peace, harmony, power and right action. Call upon the Infinite and you will get a response. You must be possessed of wisdom and guidance before you undertake any important task or decision. This is not the time to advance. Claim Divine right action is yours and then you will move forward at the right time in the right way.

*The Image*

. . . *and went up into a mountain to pray* (Luke 9:28). You climb the mountain when you contemplate the presence and power of God; the mountain represents a high state of consciousness, and when you are lifted up spiritually, all negative thoughts such as fear, resentment and anger, are dissolved in the light of God's love.

*The Lines*

Six at the bottom: *When he giveth quietness, who then can make trouble*? (Job 34:29). . . . *Peace, be still* . . . (Mark 4:39). Remember, when you seem to be in trouble, that your Higher Self abides in eternal harmony and peace. Understand there is no power in evil other than that which your thoughts give to it. Remain relaxed, quiet, and know that the law of harmony will manifest when you put behind you the thought that something can hurt you. It is wise not to advance at this time.

Six in the second place: *If thou return to the Almighty, thou shalt be built up* . . . (Job 22:23). Look to the Infinite within for the answer and the solution. Press your claim boldly with faith and confidence, refusing to take "no" for an answer, and your persistent seeking and knocking will pay dividends. The answer will come.

Nine in the third place: *The Lord will strengthen him upon the bed of languishing* . . . (Psalms 41:3). When you are tired, exhausted and mentally disturbed, turn quietly to the God-Presence within you and claim that God's river of peace and harmony is flowing through your mind, body, and all your affairs, and that what is harmony for you is harmony for all; what blesses you blesses all. Do what you know and feel to be right—this action cannot and will not hurt anybody.

Nine in the fourth place: *God is my strength and power, and he maketh my way perfect* (II Samuel 22:33). Whatever you decide to do, whether to retire from certain activities or engage in other pursuits, will be right for you, because you know it is right action for you. The man who refuses to acknowledge the guidance and direction of the Supreme Presence and Power within him is tossed about by the winds (confusion) and the waves (fear and worry).

Nine in the fifth place: *My help cometh from the Lord . . .* (Psalms 121:2). . . . *vain is the help of man* (Psalms 60:11). When you come to a decision which you know is right and good for you, pay no attention to what others think or say. Adhere to your decision, knowing that all the power and wisdom of God flows through the focal point of your decision. Listen to no man; follow the inner light of God, which shines out through you.

Nine in the sixth place: *The Lord shall guide thee continually* . . (Isaiah 58:11). You are being guided by Infinite Intelligence, and everything you do will prosper.

## 34. TA CHUANG/THE POWER OF THE GREAT

— —
— — **above Chen, The Arousing, Thunder**
——
——
—— **below Ch'ien, The Creative, Heaven**
——

### *The Judgment*

. . . *whosoever will be great among you, shall be your minister* (Mark 10:43). The great men of the world, whether they were Edison, Marconi, Einstein, or Ford, were those who contributed to the betterment of mankind. As you give service lovingly, faithfully, and continue determined to do the right thing, you will succeed.

### *The Image*

*The voice of thy thunder was in the heaven . . .* (Psalms 77:18). The "voice of thunder" in the *I Ching* and the Bible means that your

Higher Self speaks to you in the form of a desire, urging you to rise up and come on up higher. Heaven means your mind at peace. In other words, your Higher Self stirs you up from your lethargy and complacence and says to you, "God hath need of you at higher levels of expression." Know that Infinite Intelligence reveals to you the fulfillment of your plans and purposes in Divine order through Divine love.

*The Lines*

Nine at the bottom: *. . . and upon the great toe of their right foot . . .* (Exodus 29:20). "Foot" means understanding of the laws of life. You have five toes symbolic of your five senses, and if you are governed by externals such as the mass mind, conditions, events, and the like, you will experience lack and limitation. In other words, if you are giving power to any created thing and making the created greater than the Creator (your thought and feeling), you will experience failure and loss. Remember the inner controls the outer. If you let the outer control you, you will be in trouble.

Nine in the second place: *Commit thy way unto the Lord; trust also in him and he shall bring it to pass* (Psalms 37:5). This means that when you adhere strictly to the laws of your mind, an attitude ensuring that whatever you contemplate comes to pass, and you refuse to be swerved by fear or any negative suggestion, your deeper mind will respond and you will definitely be successful.

Nine in the third place: *For whosoever exalteth himself shall be abased, and he that humbleth himself shall be exalted* (Luke 14:11). You cannot really receive and hold anything except by right of consciousness, which means you have to develop the inner mental equivalent. Suppose you brag and boast and pretend to be something you are not. You are denying yourself the sure way to prominence, success and achievement. That is, you have to build inner worth, self-esteem, integrity and success into your subconscious mind through meditation and prayer. No matter how you try to push yourself forward externally, you must remember you cannot express that which you do not feel to be true within you. Stop demeaning yourself.

Nine in the fourth place: *In all thy ways acknowledge him and he shall direct thy paths* (Proverbs 3:6). Acknowledge there is an Almighty Power operating on your behalf; there is nothing to oppose

It, challenge It or vitiate It. Keep on knowing that the God-Power opens up the way for the realization of your heart's desire and all doors will open up for you now.

Six in the fifth place: . . . *every day a goat for a sin offering* . . . (Ezekiel 43:25). A goat is a symbol of sacrifice, which means you give up the lesser for the greater. For example, if you nourish a grudge, pet peeve or hostility, you will ride the goat, which means you will have negative experiences physically, mentally, financially and in all other ways. As you give up all mental antagonisms and surrender to the power and love of God, peace comes and the way opens up for you.

Six in the sixth place: . . . *and he shall separate them one from another as a shepherd divideth his sheep from the goats* (Matthew 25:32). You must play the role of the shepherd, i.e., you must separate the false from the true in your own mind. Come to a clear-cut decision in your mind that Infinite Intelligence within you is All Wise and All Powerful, and there is nothing to oppose It. Then realize that the fear and false thoughts in your mind have no reality. They are simply a conglomeration of sinister shadows with nothing to back them up. Come to a decision and realize Infinite Intelligence is opening up the way for you, and success and achievement is assured you.

## 35. Chin/Progress

———
— — **above Li, The Clinging, Fire**
———
— —
— — **below K'un, The Receptive, Earth**
— —

*The Judgment*

. . . *and the horse that the king rideth upon* . . . (Esther 6:8). The king riding upon a horse symbolizes that you are riding a mood of victory, triumph and success along all lines.

*The Image*

*Then shall the righteous shine forth as the sun* . . . (Matthew 13:43). The sun is symbolic of the Infinite Intelligence within you which lights up all the dark places of your mind. Continue to know that you are Divinely guided in all your ways, and the Light that lighteth every man that cometh into the world is a lamp unto your feet and a light upon your path.

*The Lines*

Six at the bottom: *And the Lord shall guide thee continually* . . . (Isaiah 58:11). The Lord is the Lordly power within you which is the Infinite Intelligence. Trust this Presence, believe in It, and persist in following your goal; and success will be yours.

Six in the second place: . . . *for he hath said, I will never leave thee, nor forsake thee* (Hebrews 13:5). The God-Presence is the very Life of you. This Presence is always with you; It sustains you and loves to express Itself through you. Continue to adhere to your goal in life, knowing that your subconscious will reveal to you the way and open up all doors for you, bringing you joy and peace.

Six in the third place: . . . *the way of the righteous is made plain* (Proverbs 15:19). Infinite Intelligence within your subconscious mind attracts to you all those who aid you in the realization of your objectives. The way is made plain to you through the wisdom of God, and you overcome all obstacles.

Nine in the fourth place: *The righteousness of the perfect shall direct his way: but the wicked shall fall by his own wickedness* (Proverbs 11:5). Let all that you do be done in love, honesty and integrity. Do not deviate from the principle of right action. If you take advantage or hurt another, you are only hurting yourself. Honesty is the best policy.

Six in the fifth place: *Remember ye not the former things, neither consider the things of old* (Isaiah 43:18). Remorse and worry represent spiritual blindness and an absence of faith. Waste no time in retrospection and do not waste time or energy by thinking of past errors. Change your thought and keep it changed. Rest assured that all your projects and undertakings will prosper in Divine order.

Nine in the sixth place: *I considered the horns, and behold . . .* (Daniel 7:8). Horns have been used as cups and vessels for liquids, also as trumpets. The defense of many animals is in their horns. These are symbols of strength, honor, victory and dominion. Remember, the enemies are always in your own mind. Your horn is your power to meet obstacles and to overcome them. Enter into your own mind and decisively and dynamically cast out of your mind fears, resentments, ill will and hostility. Enthrone harmony, faith, confidence and Divine right action. Don't pour out your anger on others. Insist on Divine right action from all those around you. But at the same time there must be no vindictiveness or desire to get even in your mind or heart. Let Divine law and order govern you and you will achieve victory.

## 36. Ming I/Darkening of the Light

— —<br>
— — **above K'un, The Receptive, Earth**<br>
— —<br>
——<br>
— — **below Li, The Clinging, Fire**<br>
——

*The Judgment*

. . . *God divideth the light from the darkness* (Genesis 1:4). You should always decide in your own mind the truth or falsity of any thought. To accept a negative or false thought brings trouble. Light means truth, comprehension, understanding. Affirm the good and you are dividing darkness from the light. Regardless of setbacks and problems, hold fast to the Power of God working in you and through you, and you will triumph.

*The Image*

*. . . If therefore the light that is in thee be darkness, how great is that darkness*! (Matthew 6:23). Light cannot be darkness—the meaning is, if the knowledge you have is erroneous or false and does not conform to eternal verities and principles of life, you must correct it. Get back on the beam. Realize one with God is a majority, and no one can hurt you but yourself. Give power to no person, place or thing. Bless all those around you and keep on knowing that the Light in you dispels the darkness, and the dawn appears, and all the shadows flee away.

*The Lines*

Nine at the bottom: *Let your light so shine before men that they may see your good works, and glorify your father which is in heaven* (Matthew 5:16). Become a channel for the Divine. Let the life, love, harmony and understanding of God flow through you. Exalt God in the midst of you and realize every problem is Divinely outmatched. When disharmony, discord or disappointment present themselves, be constantly aware that God is guiding you and reveals the way to achieve your goal.

Six in the second place: . . . *praises of him who hath called you out of darkness into his marvelous light* (I Peter 2:9). When in trouble or in difficulty of any kind, realize that light dispels darkness, that every problem or challenge is Divinely outmatched and as you steadfastly persist, the Infinite Power of the Infinite One will respond and aid you in overcoming and will at the same time help you to lift up all those associated with you.

Nine in the third place: *Shall thy wonders be known in the dark*? . . . (Psalms 88:12). Whatever difficulty or problem may be facing you, know that this will surely pass and that the light (your spiritual joy) will return. On a journey you may have to follow a very bad road. You may be shaken up somewhat, but there is an end to the detour. When things are rough and tough, don't act hastily or rashly. Turn toward the Light and affirm, "Victory ahead." *Be still, and know that I am God* (Psalms 46:10).

Six in the fourth place: *The words of a talebearer are as wounds, and they go down into the innermost parts of the belly* (Proverbs 26:22). The belly in the *I Ching* and the Bible means the subconscious mind. You are capable of penetrating into the darkness of the other person's mind. You are not responsible for negative patterns in the other's mind. Turn to the Healing Light within yourself. Do not get involved. Bless the other and walk on.

Six in the fifth place: *When his candle shined upon my head and when by his light I walked through darkness* (Job 29:3). Whatever type of restriction or bondage you may be in, do not fight the situation mentally. Know that Infinite Intelligence will surely open up a new door for you, leading to freedom and peace of mind. Avoid nagging at the problem from time to time all day long. Remind yourself that it is God revealing the way out through you. Persist in this attitude and you will walk through the darkness to the dawn of a new day.

Six in the sixth place: *Nor for the pestilence that walketh in darkness* . . . (Psalms 91:6). You are in darkness when you indulge in melancholia, depression, hostility or ill will. When you engage in condemnation of yourself or others, these are pestilences of the darkness. Hostile activities of others toward you reflect your emotionally disturbed state. To violate the law of harmony brings trouble. Forgive yourself and others and exalt God in the midst of you, mighty to heal.

## 37. Chia Jen/The Family (The Clan)

———
——— **above Sun, The Gentle, Wind**
— —
———
— — **below Li, The Clinging, Fire**
———

*The Judgment*

*Every wise woman buildeth her house . . .* (Proverbs 14:1). The house is your mind and you build your house by filling your mind with the truths of God, thereby growing in grace, wisdom and understanding. "Woman" in the *I Ching* is your emotional or feeling nature, the subjective side of you. When the conscious and subconscious synchronize, harmonize and unite on the spiritual values of life, the children of that union are harmony, peace, abundance, vitality, health and security. The same applies on the objective plane. When a husband and wife love each other and exalt God in one another, the marriage grows more progressively blessed through the years.

*The Image*

*. . . wind fulfilling his word* (Psalms 148:8). "Wind" means the Spirit in you. The words which you speak should be from your heart; that is to say, they should be felt as true, backed up by your conviction that what you say is true. The Bible says, *. . . the words that I speak unto you, they are spirit and they are life* (John 6:63).

*The Lines*

Nine at the bottom: *And the ark of God remained with the family . . . and the Lord blessed the house . . .* (I Chronicles 13:14). The ark of God represents God's love uniting all members of the family. There is no love without discipline and no discipline without love. Parents who love their children will insist that the children do that which is right and will see that they have a reverence for the spiritual values of life, such as the Ten Commandments, the Golden Rule, and the Law of Love. Children grow up in the image and likeness of the dominant mental and spiritual climate of the home.

Six in the second place: . . . *and a prudent wife is from the Lord* (Proverbs 19:14). One of the meanings of the word wife is that to which you are mentally and emotionally united. It is also your subconscious mind. If you are a woman, you should see to it that you are not being impregnated by five-sense propaganda and the fears, doubts and negatives of the mass mind. Nourish and feed your mind with inspiration, confidence, faith, love, goodwill and an absolute conviction of the goodness of God in the land of the living.

Nine in the third place: *And to knowledge temperance; and to temperance patience; and to patience godliness* (II Peter 1:6). An occasional outburst of temper between husband and wife or brother and sister is not bad. It is the sustained grudge or pet peeve or suppressed rage that creates havoc. It would be a very insipid marriage without an occasional quarrel. When this is of momentary duration and a little later all is forgotten and forgiven, no harm results. Moderation, or self-restraint in action and self-control of thoughts and emotions, is essential for a happy life. Moderation for you in all things is indicated.

Six in the fourth place: *In the house of the righteous is much treasure* . . . (Proverbs 15:6). The treasure house of infinity is within your subconscious, which is one with Infinite Intelligence and boundless wisdom. You are releasing these treasures when you claim that God is now being expressed through your thoughts, words and deeds, during every hour of the day. Great success and abundance are assured you.

Nine in the fifth place: . . . *Thou sayest that I am a King* . . . (John 18:37). You are a king when you take charge of your thoughts, imagery, emotions and reactions and direct all of them along God-like ways. You are a king over your conceptive realm, as you have complete dominion in directing your mental and spiritual forces. As you enthrone peace, harmony and love in your mind, you will radiate goodwill to all, and whatever you undertake will prosper, and many blessings are yours.

Nine in the sixth place: . . . *that we might work the works of God?* (John 6:28). Let everything that you do be done in loving kindness. Character is destiny, and as you do everything for the glory of God, wonders happen in your life. Success and prosperity are assured you.

## 38. K'UEI/OPPOSITION

———

— — **above Li, The Clinging, Flame**

———

— —

——— **below Tui, The Joyous, Lake**

———

### *The Judgment*

. . . *with thy strong hand thou opposest thyself against me* (Job 30:21). The difference between success and failure is simply the conflict between the idea of success and the idea of failure in your own mind. You are born to succeed. The Infinite cannot fail. Sing the song of triumph and accomplishment in your mind. Back up the idea of success with faith and enthusiasm, and your subconscious mind will react accordingly and compel you to succeed, and any idea of failure will die in your mind. The opposition is always in your mind. Our thoughts come in pairs. One must die that the other may live. The opposites in life are halves of the one whole. The reconciliation of the opposites brings peace and harmony, such as the harmonious union of man and woman.

*The Image*

*. . . we went through fire and through water; but thou broughtest us out into a wealthy place* (Psalms 66:12). "Fire" and "water" represent respectively the fires of passion or excitation, and emotional upheavals and disturbances. Remember, in all such cases, that the Infinite Intelligence in your subconscious mind will lead you out of any difficulties. God's river of peace calms the waters, and Divine love restores your mind to a state of serenity and poise. Never permit others to drag you down to the level of anger and resentment. Remain in tune with the Infinite and all will be well.

*The Lines*

Nine at the bottom: *Hast thou given the horse strength?* . . . (Job 39:19). The horse is a means of transportation and is symbolic of your mood, your emotional nature which propels you to your goal. If your emotions are disturbed by the actions or statements of others, be sure to avoid criticism, resentment and attempts to get even with unfortunates with warped minds. To do so would cause you to descend to the same mental frequency, and you would become enmeshed thereby in the negative vibrations of the others. Remain aloof and undisturbed, and Divine understanding will prevail.

Nine in the second place: *. . . my soul doth magnify the Lord* (Luke 1:46). The Lord is the Lordly Power of God within you, but psychologically your lord is also the dominant idea which controls your mind. Like attracts like, and according to the law of attraction you will attract the person or meet the type of individual who is uppermost in your mind. This is simply the law of mind in action.

Six in the third place: *And Moses took the wagons and the oxen* . . . (Numbers 7:6). The inner meaning of "Moses" is that of a man who draws out the wisdom and power of God from his subconscious mind and then moves forward to his goal and to victory. The oxen and wagons represent beasts of burden who carry the load for you to your destination. Your subconscious powers will carry the load for you if you trust them completely. They will lead you to your objective when you meet with reverses and setbacks, and when others criticize or mock you. Remain calm. Cling to your inner guidance and know that through the wisdom and power of your subconscious you will attain a Divine harmonious solution, and you will experience a happy ending.

Nine in the fourth place: *And when they opposed themselves . . .* (Acts 18:6). The opposition is always in your own mind. You can resolve any problem and reconcile the opposites in your mind by prayer. Prayer is contemplating the truths of God from the highest standpoint. Realize that Infinite Intelligence attracts to you the associates you seek, and you will get a response. The law of affinity will work for you, and you will receive an answer which satisfies you.

Six in the fifth place: *Remember ye not the former things, neither consider the things of old* (Isaiah 43:18). The past is dead. Nothing matters but this moment. Change your present thought and you change your destiny. The future is your present thinking made manifest. Your new mental attitude of faith and confidence breaks through all barriers and obstacles, insuring success for you.

Nine in the sixth place: . . . *and he sent him into his fields to feed swine* (Luke 15:15). The pig in the *I Ching* and in our Bible represents an unclean state of mind. When you have an unconscious sense of guilt and a psychic boil within and subsequently fear rejection, such as when you think that others are unresponsive to you, your fear and sensitiveness cause you to project hostility and animosity on to others. In other words, you are projecting your own inner turmoil on to others. The trouble is within yourself. Affirm boldly: "God's love fills my soul and God's peace flows through my mind. God's light reveals the way, and the sunshine of His love goes before me preparing my path." As you do this, God will rain blessings upon you, and you will experience peace and harmony in this changing world.

## 39. Chien/Obstruction

— —

—— **above K'an, The Abysmal, Water**

— —

——

— — **below Ken, Keeping Still, Mountain**

— —

### *The Judgment*

. . . *there is no power but of God* . . . (Romans 13:1). When some difficulty presents itself, become aware of the power of the Infinite within you. Be patient. Seek spiritual counsel. Do not mentally fight the situation. Infinite Intelligence knows the way over all hurdles. *The Lord shall fight for you, and ye shall hold your peace* (Exodus 14:14). A harmonious solution takes place.

### *The Image*

*Counsel in the heart of man is like deep water* . . . (Proverbs 20:5). The heart in the *I Ching* and in the Bible symbolizes your subconscious mind. It is also referred to as deep water. You can receive guidance from your deep water by affirming: "Infinite Intelligence reveals to me the answer and shows me the way I should go. I follow the *lead* which comes to me." Remember, the problem, the difficulty, is in your mind and must be solved there. You can rise above any challenge, knowing that through your contact with the Divine Presence all things are possible to him that believeth.

### *The Lines*

Six at the bottom: . . . *wait on the Lord, and he shall save thee* (Proverbs 20:22). The Lord represents the power and wisdom of your subconscious mind. To wait means to relax, to let go, and to cease all struggle and mental resistance. Claim: "Divine right action governs all my actions, and the Guiding Principle within me reveals to my conscious mind the next step at the right time in the right way, and I wait in faith and expectancy, knowing right action prevails."

Six in the second place: . . . *sent his angel to shew unto his servants the things which must shortly be done* (Revelation 22:6). Your "servants" are your thoughts, ideas, mental images, desires. These must obey you when you use the law of your mind in the right way. Go forth to meet your problem. Realize it is Divinely outmatched. Hold steadily to the Power and Wisdom of God in spite of difficulties, and you will find yourself in safety. Be aware of the Love and Presence of God. This awareness is a protection against danger.

Nine in the third place: *In all thy ways acknowledge him, and he shall direct thy paths* (Proverbs 3:6). Turn within to the Indwelling Presence and claim that you are Divinely directed. Do not make a frontal assault; fly over the problem mentally and understand that God knows and God cares for you. Remain calm and poised, and realize that now is the time to remain quiet in your own home, trusting the Divine Presence to govern you in all ways.

Six in the fourth place: *Great peace have they which love thy law: and nothing shall offend them* (Psalms 119:165). All you have to do is to realize the presence of Infinite Intelligence and Boundless Wisdom within your own subconscious mind. Do what you have to do to the best of your ability and keep your mind fixed on the Infinite Intelligence within, Which leads and guides you until the storm is over. This is the time to remain quiet in God, and you will attract all those who will aid you in achieving your goal.

Nine in the fifth place: *A friend loveth at all times* . . . (Proverbs 17:17). Your greatest friend in the world is God—the Life Principle within you. This Presence made you, created you and now sustains you. God never deserts His creation. Join up with God and realize with God that all things are possible and further realize you can do all t ings through the God-Power which strengtheneth you. You will attract all those who will assist you to fulfill your dreams.

Six at the top: *Acquaint now thyself with him and be at peace* . . . (Job 22:21). You can get acquainted with the God-Presence by tuning in on the Infinite now, and feel His river of peace flowing through you. Claim God is guiding you to do the right thing. You are here to serve and to give of your talents to the world. You are living in a subjective and an objective world, and you should seek counsel and advice from someone you trust who can aid you objectively to fulfill your desire. Success and prosperity are assured you.

## 40. Hsieh/Deliverance

— —
— — **above Chen, The Arousing, Thunder**
——
— —
—— **below K'an, The Abysmal, Water**
— —

*The Judgment*

*. . . to preach deliverance to the captives . . . to set at liberty them that are bruised* (Luke 4:18). There is an Infinite Healing Presence within you that lifts you up, heals, restores, guides and directs you. This Presence frees you from bondage and limitation and sets you on the high road to freedom and peace of mind. Divine law and order are operating in your life, and whatever you do will prosper. There is no under action or over action, only right action.

*The Image*

*And when ye stand praying: forgive, if ye have ought against any* . . . (Mark 11:25). Forgiveness means you must wish the other person well. You must forgive hurts and injuries sincerely in your heart so that when you think about them, there is no longer any sting in your mind. Forgiveness does not mean to make a "doormat" of yourself. Resentment and a desire to see someone punished rot your soul and fasten your troubles to you like rivets. Forgive yourself also for harboring negative thoughts, and as you release the other person or persons, you make way for the river of life, love, truth and abundance to flow into your experience.

*The Lines*

Six at the bottom: . . . *God is love; and he that dwelleth in love dwelleth in God, and God in him* (I John 4:16). Your sense of love and goodwill rebuilds your body; brings inspiration, inner peace and serenity; and opens the way for expansion along all lines.

Nine in the second place: . . . *the little foxes that spoil the vines* . . . (Song of Solomon 2:15). The foxes represent any sly, deceptive, cunning attitudes of mind. There must be no ulterior motive of any kind. Dissolve negative emotions by realizing that God's love fills your soul, and wish for everyone what you wish for yourself. Know that you can solve your problem with prayer, justice and goodwill, and, thereby, you will definitely succeed.

Six in the third place: *For whosoever exalteth himself shall be abased; and he that humbleth himself shall be exalted* (Luke 14:11). Do not pretend to be that which you are not. You can't possess anything except by right of consciousness. You must build the mental equivalent of that which you want to be into your mentality. The extent to which you are trying to push yourself forward aggressively in order to achieve prominence among men, will determine the degree of your failure. In order to be important in the world, you must have inner worth, integrity and character. The law of your subconscious will place you where you should be regardless of all your conscious striving. You become what you contemplate and feel as true in your heart—nothing more or less.

Nine in the fourth place: . . . *and upon the great toes of their right feet* . . . (Leviticus 8:24). "Feet" means understanding, and the "right" means the objective world or the world of the five senses. You must not judge according to appearances. Your "big toe" means you are being governed by your five senses, and you are moving forward in your mind in the wrong way. Detach yourself completely from appearances and the five-sense evidence and false impressions of the mass mind and know that God is your Senior Partner. The God-Presence leads and guides you in all ways. You will thereby attract to yourself the right associates in Divine order.

Six in the fifth place: . . . *faith without works is dead* (James 2:20). You must demonstrate your faith in God and in all things good. Come to a clear-cut decision in your mind to eradicate the negative patterns there. What you neglect and ignore in your mind fades away and dies because you starved it mentally and emotionally. Build harmony, peace, right action, and prosperity into your subconscious, and the unwanted things and unwelcome people will disappear.

Six in the sixth place: *But these are they of which ye shall not eat* . . . (Deuteronomy 14:12). . . . *and the hawk after his kind* (Deuteronomy 14:15). The hawk is a bird of prey and, symbolically speaking, you should not prey on other men or take advantage of them in any way whatsoever. It is said that men pray together on Sunday and prey on each other on Monday. Kill any ulterior motive in your mind, and make sure that your motivation and actions are based on the Golden Rule and the Law of Love. As you do this, everything you undertake will certainly prosper.

## 41. SUN/DECREASE

——<br>
— — **above Ken, Keeping Still, Mountain**<br>
— —<br>
— —<br>
—— **below Tui, The Joyous, Lake**<br>
——

*The Judgment*

*He must increase, but I must decrease* (John 3:30). This means intuition, or the wisdom of God, must increase and grow, and your intellectual, materialistic concept of life must diminish. Claim that your intellect is anointed with the wisdom of God; then you will use your conscious, reasoning mind to carry out the dictates of the Divine within you. Your body, your environment and conditions are plastic to your thoughts, and externals always reflect your sincere beliefs. Dwell mentally on prosperity, abundance and securing God's riches, and your habitual thinking will be experienced.

*The Image*

*He that is slow to anger is better than the mighty; and he that ruleth his spirit than he that taketh a city* (Proverbs 16:32). In order that you might lead a full and happy life, control of your emotions is essential. To govern and control your emotions, it is essential to maintain control over your thoughts. You can't find peace any other way. Willpower or coercion will not do it. The answer is to enthrone God-like thoughts in your mind. Busy yourself mentally with the concepts of peace, harmony and goodwill, and His inner peace will lead you to still waters and green pastures.

*The Lines*

Nine at the bottom: . . . *fulfill your works, your daily tasks* . . . (Exodus 5:13). You are here to express yourself fully, to find your true place in life, and to contribute your talents for the benefit of humanity. You are a part of the great ocean of mankind, and you are here to do your share. Unselfish assistance to others is good, provided you help others to help themselves. Remember, each man is here to learn to discover his hidden powers and stand on his own feet, solving his problems manfully by himself. A man who receives help too easily ceases to propel himself and becomes a leaner instead of a lifter.

Nine in the second place: *Thou wilt keep him in perfect peace, whose mind is stayed on thee* . . . (Isaiah 26:3). This is a time to focus your attention on things Divine and to listen to the inner voice of intuition. Do not undertake any task until your mind is completely at peace and you have that inner silent knowledge that it is the right thing to do. You have to be extremely careful how you help another person. Teach him of his own Divinity and how to tap his inner powers of the subconscious mind, and he won't need any other kind of assistance from you. Do not dissipate your energy foolishly.

Six in the third place: . . . *take nothing for your journey* . . . (Luke 9:3). This means to take faith in God in your heart wherever you go. You are always travelling in your mind from a problem to a solution. The journey is always decided in the mind first. Whatever you are praying about, keep it to yourself and do not discuss it with others. Keep your own counsel and "go and tell no man." Sometimes when you talk about your plans, aspirations or desires to others, they may tend to ridicule your prayers, or talk you out of them. Moreover, you may stir up envy. Keep your plans secret and discuss them with no one. Know that your Divine Companion is God and that God and His Wisdom are bringing about the realization of your heart's desire and all your plans will turn out well.

Six in the fourth place: . . . *cleanse thou me from secret faults* (Psalms 19:12). When you give your mental assent to any idea, good or bad, you must realize that you are depositing the idea into your subconscious—to the extent that you feel it. You eradicate your faults by giving your assent mentally to love, goodwill, kindness, harmony, peace, Divine right action and good humor. As you dwell on these truths you will incorporate them into your experience, and you will benefit along all lines—socially, financially and in your home life.

Six in the fifth place: *For whosoever shall call upon the name of the Lord shall be saved* (Romans 10:13). The "name" means the nature of God, and God is All Powerful—the only power there is. One with God is a majority. There is nothing to oppose the Supreme Power. Turn to the God-Presence quietly, with faith and confidence, and affirm that God is opening up your path and solving your problem. Remind yourself that to Him nothing is impossible and great blessings will be yours.

Nine in the sixth place: . . . *but God that giveth the increase* (I Corinthians 3:7). God is the source of all things. Align yourself with the Infinite One and affirm boldly: "God multiplies my good exceedingly, and His riches flow to me freely, joyously and lovingly," and you will be richly blessed. The more wisdom you give, the more you have; the more love and goodwill you radiate, the more you possess. What blesses you blesses all. As you walk the earth with the praise of God and the harmony of God in your heart, all men are blessed, because you walk this way.

## 42. I/Increase

——<br>
—— **above Sun, The Gentle, Wind**<br>
— —<br>
— —<br>
— — **below Chen, The Arousing, Thunder**<br>
——

*The Judgment*

*. . . the Lord thy God shall bless thee in all thine increase, and in all the works of thine hands, therefore thou shalt surely rejoice* (Deuteronomy 16:15). God is guiding and prospering you in all ways, and it is to your advantage to make a decision now for further growth, expansion and personal unfoldment, and whatever you do will prosper.

*The Image*

*. . . the joy of the Lord is your strength* (Nehemiah 8:10). Life is a progression, an endless unfoldment up the ladder of life. It is not an unbroken progress up the steps of life. We move forward for

a while and then perhaps we suffer a little setback, whereby we consolidate our power and wisdom for the next advance. The real movement of your life is upward. You will rise higher much more quickly when you cremate and burn up all negative thoughts and fears in your mind with the fire of Divine love.

*The Lines*

Nine at the bottom: *Except the Lord build the house, they labour in vain that build it . . .* (Psalms 127:1). Real success and achievement in life comes from inspiration. The power and wisdom of God are now flowing through you. It is perfectly all right for you to work hard, but do not make hard work of it. You are inspired from On High, and whatever you undertake now will prosper in a wonderful way.

Six in the second place: *For as he thinketh in his heart, so is he . . .* (Proverbs 23:7). The law of your mind is that whatever you impress on your subconscious mind will come to pass. The heart means your subconscious mind, and thinking in the heart means that the thoughts and ideas which are emotionalized and felt as true will be objectified. Your subconscious magnifies whatever is deposited in it. Contemplate what is lovely and of good report. As you sense your oneness with God, there is no power in Heaven or on earth to withhold success from you.

Six in the third place: *Be still, and know that I an. God . . .* (Psalms 46:10). Quiet the wheels of your mind and remind yourself that God indwells you. Whenever you experience a setback or a disappointment, pronounce it as good. Affirm it is God in action, meaning all around harmony and peace, and the event will turn out to be a blessing in disguise. Join up with the Infinite in the same way as an operator uses an electric hoist to lift the load, just by turning on a switch and leaving it on. The electric power without any struggle lifts the load to any desired height. Let the God-Power work through you, and your faith will be amply rewarded.

Six in the fourth place: *Wherefore by their fruits ye shall know them* (Matthew 7:20). The secret of your advancement and promotion to high places is to believe that God is working through you in whatever you may be doing. Desire to serve first. Be sincere, practical, and as efficient as you can. You will be surprised at the results. Others put trust in you and you will be exalted.

Nine in the fifth place: *And be ye kind one to another . . .* (Ephesians 4:32). Kindness is a child of love. Love and kindness exist in your heart. Love dissolves everything unlike itself. The kindness of your heart is subjectively received by others, and they respond accordingly. There is an old saying, which runs as follows: "When you don't know what to do, do the kind thing." Kindness is the outcome of love. "Politeness is to do and say the kindest thing in the kindest way." Wonderful blessings are in store for you. All good is yours.

Nine in the sixth place: *We then that are strong ought to bear the infirmities of the weak, and not to please ourselves. Let every one of us please his neighbour for his good to edification* (Romans 15:1–2). You are a part of the great mass of humanity, and you must understand that you owe your success and achievement in large part to others. If in business, people bought your products and supported you. Likewise, you are here to contribute to others wisely, generously, judiciously and lovingly. Take part in the betterment of your neighbor and give up morbid selfishness. Pour out love and goodwill to all. Keep in tune with the Infinite and do that which is lawful and right. When you deviate from the Divine law of harmony, you bring trouble and loss into your experience.

## 43. Kuai/Break-through (Resoluteness)

**above Tui, The Joyous, Lake**

**below Ch'ien, The Creative, Heaven**

*The Judgment*

*. . . in quietness and in confidence shall be your strength . . .* (Isaiah 30:15). In the prayer process *effort defeats itself*. The more stress and strain you indulge in mentally, the less will be your end result. This is the opposite of the physical plane. The faster you drive your car the sooner will you reach your destination. The exact opposite, however, is the case with your thought life. Mental pressure is foredoomed to failure. When your mind is tense and angry, your deeper mind does not respond creatively. Relax, realize that you overcome evil with good. Join up with the Infinite ocean of God's love within you and know that God's love dissolves everything unlike itself. This attitude enables you to reach your goal.

*The Image*

*There is that scattereth, and yet increaseth; and there is that withholdeth more than is meet, but it tendeth to poverty* (Proverbs 11:24). This means the more you give wisely the more you have. Millionaires give away millions for useful and constructive purposes to benefit humanity, and countless millions come back to them. It is like putting seeds into the ground; they return a hundredfold or a thousandfold. Give constructively and wisely, making sure the gift uplifts humanity and is generally beneficial. This means give of your wisdom, your knowledge, your mental acumen, and also your material wealth. Do all this under the guidance of God.

*The Lines*

Nine at the beginning: *For which of you, intending to build a tower, sitteth not down first, and counteth the cost, whether he have sufficient to finish it?* (Luke 14:28). This is a part of a parable, and there is an inside meaning to all parables. We must see the hidden meaning; otherwise, it is of no value. For example, if you are ill or have a growth in your body and it does not dissolve through prayer, you should see a doctor or surgeon immediately. Bless him and eradicate the condition. If you can grow a tooth through prayer, well and good; if you can't, go to a dentist at once. Likewise, if you want to build a new home and have the absolute, unqualified faith that all the money needed will be yours and that it will be finished in Divine order, you will succeed. A longing and pining for faith is not true faith. If you don't have the necessary faith, wait until you have the money, then build.

Nine in the second place: *There is no fear in love; but perfect love casteth out fear . . .* (I John 4:18). Fear is faith in the wrong thing. Fear is a shadow in your mind. Fear is faith upside down, or God upside down. God is the only Presence and Power, and God is love. "Love worketh no ill." You lose fear to the degree you give allegiance, loyalty and devotion to the Infinite Power within you. There is nothing in God's universe to fear. Fear is a thought in your mind. Supplant it with faith in God and all things good, and when fear knocks at the door of your mind, there is no one there.

Nine in the third place: *. . . for thou hast smitten all mine enemies upon the cheek bone . . .* (Psalms 3:7). The "cheek bone" represents your conscious mind. The enemies are thoughts of fear and limitation in your conscious mind. The Psalmist says: *He shall not be afraid of evil tidings; his heart is fixed, trusting in the Lord* (Psalms 112:7). Keep your faith in God steadfast. Give power to no one, but the Infinite within you. Realize no one can hurt you, because you are a follower and are faithful to that which is good and true.

Nine in the fourth place: *And he hath on his . . . thigh a name written, King of Kings and Lord of Lords* (Revelation 19:16). *Because I knew that thou art obstinate . . .* (Isaiah 48:4). "Thigh" is a euphemistic word for the creative organs of man, which is a phallic symbol for the Creative Power of God in man. When you lack faith and confidence, you hesitate and become incapable of moving forward. Do not be obstinate and self-willed. Willpower is useless when it comes to prayer, and it gets you nowhere.

Nine in the fifth place: *. . . the weeds were wrapped about my head* (Jonah 2:5). "Weeds" represent negative, fearful thoughts which cling tenaciously. Come to a clear-cut decision and refuse to entertain negative thoughts. When they come to your mind, which they will because of habit, supplant them immediately with constructive thoughts. After a while they will lose all momentum and you will reach your goal.

Six in the sixth place: *But he that endure unto the end, the same shall be saved* (Matthew 24:13). It is necessary for you to constantly watch and destroy all negative thoughts of fear, doubt, and resentment. These corrode the soul. Constant mental discipline is essential. Eternal vigilance is the price of freedom from lack, loss and limitation. To refuse to persist in this manner denotes loss.

## 44. Kou/Coming to Meet

**above Ch'ien, The Creative, Heaven**

**below Sun, The Gentle, Wind**

*The Judgment*

*The fire consumed their young men, and their maidens were not given to marriage* (Psalms 78:63). "Fire" represents passion and lust. Marriage for any reason other than love is not a real marriage. Divine love should unite two hearts together. Each should harmonize with the other. A maiden also means any emotional state, and if your aims are based on ulterior motives of any kind, you should not enter into any contract. Moreover, if someone approaches you with any sort of a proposition, it would be wise to forego it. A contract of any kind should be based on honesty and should be mutually satisfactory.

*The Image*

*The wind bloweth where it listeth . . .* (John 3:8). The wind represents the movement of the Spirit in you. Whatever you claim and feel to be true will come to pass in all phases of your life. Your subconscious brings forth as experiences and conditions all that is impressed upon it.

*The Lines*

Six at the bottom: *I have heard the check of my reproach, and the spirit of my understanding causeth me to answer* (Job 20:3). If you are upbraiding or censuring anyone or if you feel resentful, this attitude will block your good and bring you loss. Cremate and burn up any ugly emotion within you with the fires of Divine Love and external goodwill to all.

Nine in the second place: *Or if he ask a fish will he give him a serpent?* (Matthew 7:10). "Fish" symbolizes the fact that you can fish any idea, solution or answer to any problem out of your subconscious mind if you are a good fisherman, meaning if you quiet your mind, immobilize your attention and ask for the answer. If you are receptive, the fish (idea) will well up from your subconscious into your conscious, reasoning mind. Be sure you fish out the mood of love, goodwill and peace from your subconscious and radiate that feeling to all those around you.

Nine in the third place: . . . *on his thigh a name written* . . . (Revelation 19:16). The thigh symbolizes the creative organs of man, which from a phallic standpoint means the male and female principle within you, i.e., your conscious and subconscious mind. When it is said there is no skin on your thigh, it means you are not being covered by faith and confidence in the One Power, and you are being disturbed by external conditions. Redirect your emotions along God-like channels and get back on the beam of Divine right action.

Nine in the fourth place: . . . *bring of the fish which ye have now caught* (John 21:10). It is essential if you wish to gain cooperation and loyalty of people that you fish out of the depths of yourself Divine guidance, right action and harmony. Draw out of your subconscious the mood of goodwill, kindness and cooperation with people. In that way you prevent loss and limitation.

Nine in the fifth place: *We remember the fish . . . and the melons* . . . (Numbers 11:5). Melons are a delicious fruit in a hot climate and were among the articles of food for which the Hebrews pined in the desert. This symbolizes the fruits of the Spirit in you, which are love, joy, peace, quietness, faith, humility and goodwill to all. What you radiate comes back to you pressed down, shaken together and running over.

Nine in the sixth place: . . . *these are the horns which have scattered Judah* . . . (Zechariah 1:19). "Horns" represent power, and Judah means exaltation of God. There is only One Power, and when you use this Power the wrong way, you get into trouble in all phases of your life. Stop fighting conditions in your mind or you will scatter your forces and deplete your vitality.

## 45. Ts'ui/Gathering Together (Massing)

— —
——— above Tui, The Joyous, Lake
———
— —
— — below K'un, The Receptive, Earth
— —

*The Judgment*

. . . *how often would I have gathered thy children together, even as a hen gathereth her chickens under her wings* . . . (Matthew 23:37). Gather all your thoughts, ideas and plans together and know that you are in the Presence of God, and as the hen gathers the chickens under her wings, covering them with her feathers from all possible harm and hurt, in the same manner will the God-Presence protect, guide and guard you once you have decided to place your faith in the Only Presence, Cause, and Power—namely, God within you—the Living Spirit Almighty. The sacrifice you make is simply to give all your allegiance and loyalty to God alone.

*The Image*

*Elect according to the foreknowledge of God* . . . (I Peter 1:2). The leader in your mind, or the dominant conviction, should be your belief in the guidance of Infinite Intelligence in all your decisions. Pray for guidance before making important decisions. Claim you are being Divinely directed, *and believe it*; and the ultimate outcome will be good even if things don't go to your liking for a time, provided you really believe what you affirm. Do what seems right at the time, taking all circumstances into consideration, and your feeling of right action will be communicated to others and will bless all associated with you.

*The Lines*

Six at the bottom: . . . *if we hold fast the confidence and the rejoicing of the hope firm unto the end* (Hebrews 3:6). Be faithful to the end. Trust the Infinite Intelligence to guide you all the way. Do not waver and vacillate, as this leads to a double-minded state. Picture the happy ending, and through the powers of your subconscious, which respond to your affirmative attitude, you will succeed.

Six in the second place: . . . *and all were drawn up again into heaven* (Acts 11:10). "Heaven" means your mind at peace and in tune with the Infinite. The law of attraction is working for you. Infinite Intelligence attracts to you all those who harmonize with you. Trust the principle of right action and you will prosper in your undertakings.

Six in the third place: . . . *they shall obtain joy and gladness, and sorrow and sighing shall flee away* (Israel 35:10). In times of sorrow or grief, realize that everything eventually passes away. Do not give power to others to upset you in any way. Maintain your equilibrium. Join up with the God-Presence within you and realize you are always in your true place and doing the works of Him that sent you. Keep going forward, and no one can block your good. Divine right action is yours now.

Nine in the fourth place: *I am glad of the coming of Stephanas and Fortunatus* . . . (I Corinthians 16:17). "Stephanas" means you are crowned with victory. "Fortunatus" means spiritual, mental and material riches flow to you now.

Nine in the fifth place: . . . *all things work together for good to them that love God* . . . (Romans 8:28). You love God when you refuse to give any power to externals or to other people. Give all your allegiance and devotion to the One Power, realizing there is no other power to oppose the One and Only Power. Adhere to the principles of truth, integrity, honesty and right action, and all those who may not agree with you will be constrained to do you honor and good.

Six in the sixth place: *And God shall wipe away all tears* . . . (Revelation 21:4). Your tears pass away. Let nothing disturb you, let nothing annoy you, let nothing sadden you. Everything passes away but God, and God alone is sufficient. Surrender to the Divine Presence within you and know that it is God in action, which means all around harmony and peace in your life, and the results will be good.

## 46. SHENG/PUSHING UPWARD

— —

— — **above K'un, The Receptive, Earth**

— —

———

——— **below Sun, The Gentle, Wind, Wood**

— —

*The Judgment*

*Who knoweth the spirit of man that goeth upward* . . . (Ecclesiastes 3:21). The Spirit of God animates, sustains and strengthens you. Know that God is guiding you to the right counselor who will aid and assist you in the right way. You are Divinely active, and whatever you do will prosper in a wonderful way.

*The Image*

*Let the field be joyful and all that is therein: then shall all the trees of the wood rejoice* (Psalms 96:12). The roots of the trees absorb all the chemicals and moisture from the soil necessary for their growth. This is based on a subjective wisdom operating automatically, and the tendency of all trees is to move upward toward the heavens. Likewise, as you move forward with faith and confidence you will attract everything necessary for the unfoldment or blossoming of your plans, and you will be very successful.

*The Lines*

Six at the bottom: This means that . . . *in quietness and in confidence shall be your strength* . . . (Isaiah 30:15). This indicates that whatever plans you have, you should go forward with the absolute conviction that great blessings are yours—right now.

Nine in the second place: . . . *serve him in sincerity and in truth* . . . (Joshua 24:14). Being free from deceit and falseness of all kinds and adhering to honesty, integrity and justice favor your success. The offering and sacrifices mentioned in the *I Ching* and in our Bible mean giving up the lesser for the greater. For example, if you speak rudely, begin to speak kindly and lovingly—that will be an offering and a sacrifice.

Nine in the third place: *No good thing will he withhold from them that walk uprightly* (Psalms 84:11). As you move forward joyously and confidently, all the powers of God move on your behalf, and you are assured of success and prosperity in your undertakings.

Six in the fourth place: *I will sing unto the Lord, because he hath dealt bountifully with me* (Psalms 13:6). Keep going forward, be joyous and happy, and give thanks to the Source of all blessings. Honor and promotion are bestowed on you.

Six in the fifth place: . . . *and bring forth fruit with patience* (Luke 8:15). Suppress restlessness and annoyance in waiting. Have persistent courage in difficult circumstances. Growth is by degrees. It is the quiet, peaceful mind, full of confidence, that gets things done. You will advance in a wonderful way, though gradually and by degrees in Divine order.

Six in the sixth place: *To give light to them that sit in darkness . . . to guide our feet unto the way of peace* (Luke 1:79). Darkness is absence of light. "Light" means Infinite Intelligence within you that knows the way out of darkness (problems, difficulties, obstructions). Trust implicitly the Infinite Intelligence within your subconscious to lead and guide you in all ways. Adhere to the great truth that all problems are Divinely outmatched. Do not fight problems or difficulties in your mind, as this attitude would make matters worse. Follow the Guiding Principle within you. It always speaks in peace, never in confusion.

## 47. K'UN/OPPRESSION (EXHAUSTION)

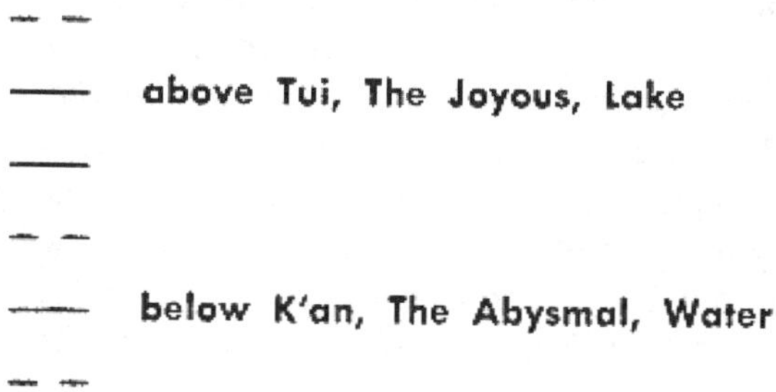


*The Judgment*

*If thou faint in the day of adversity, thy strength is small* (Proverbs 24:10). Stand up to every problem or challenging situation in life. Face it and conquer it through the power and wisdom of God in you. Be clear-sighted, practical and understanding. You have an opportunity to draw out the powers of your subconscious mind, and then you find out the kind of stuff you are made of, and also you discover that the great joy is in overcoming. There is that within you which is stronger than anything outside of you. Be still, quiet and confident, and you will succeed.

*The Image*

. . . *and the water thereof was dried up* . . . (Revelation 16:12). When you are not in tune with the Infinite and when you fail to drink of inspiration, faith, confidence, guidance and courage which can only come from aligning yourself with the Infinite, then the waters have dried up in you. You must replenish your mental and spiritual batteries and remain faithful to the power of the Indwelling Presence *He restoreth my soul* . . . (Psalms 23:3).

*The Lines*

Six at the bottom: *Trust not in oppression* . . . (Psalms 62:10). When you feel oppressed, depressed and melancholy, remember that dwelling in such a mental atmosphere compounds and magnifies your misery. Whatever you focus your attention on is magnified by your subconscious, and if it is negative, it induces failure. Go and seek a good counselor and get mental and spiritual advice.

Nine in the second place: *For the Kingdom of heaven is not meat and drink, but righteousness and peace and joy in the Holy Ghost* (Romans 14:17). You can eat the choicest food yet be sick, frustrated, depressed and unhappy. You must receive and partake of spiritual food regularly by praying repetitiously, an act which consists of filling your mind with the concepts of harmony, right action, peace, joy, love and inspiration from On High. Call upon the Infinite Intelligence and It will respond to you. Do not undertake any project until you have prayed about it and feel right about it in your own heart.

Six in the third place: *Thorns, also thistles shall it bring forth to thee* . . . (Genesis 3:18). . . . *Take ye away the stone* . . . (John 11:39). The stone represents a hard, unyielding and inflexible state of mind based on ignorance, fear and superstition. A stone could also be an acute state of depression which you are unwilling to release. Thorns and thistles represent irritations and resentments which sting you and rob you of vitality, enthusiasm and energy. This attitude of mind attracts loss and failure. You must forgive yourself and everybody else before you can get a healing.

Nine in the fourth place: *Deliver me from the oppression of man*

. . . (Psalms 119:134). You are delivered from your problems when you place your confidence in the right place, namely, the God-Presence within you, Which knows all and sees all and Which has the know-how of accomplishment. Affirm: "God is guiding me in all ways and the power of the Almighty backs me up." You will reach your objective in life in Divine order.

Nine in the fifth place: . . . *They shall take away thy nose* . . . (Ezekiel 23:25). Your nose represents your skill at discernment, your judgment or decisions. A dog smells unsavory food and rejects it. Likewise, you must separate the false from the true. Having come to the conclusion that there is only one Power—the Living Spirit within—you turn to this Presence and claim harmony, peace, right action, and the joy of the Lord which is your strength. As you do, the day breaks for you and all the shadows flee away.

Six in the sixth place: *Remember ye not the former things, neither consider the things of old* (Isaiah 43:18). Forget the past. The past is dead; nothing lives but this moment. Change your present thought and keep it changed, and you will change your destiny. If you are thinking of grudges, peeves and hurts, you are thinking of them now and reinfecting yourself. The future is your present thought made manifest. Forgive yourself for harboring negative thoughts and resolve to refrain from such weakness from now on. Forgive others also. There is no use crying over spilt milk. Come to a definite conclusion in your mind that you are moving forward in a new direction, and everything you do will prosper.

## 48. CHING/THE WELL

— —<br>
——— **above K'an, The Abysmal, Water**<br>
— —<br>
———<br>
——— **below Sun, The Gentle, Wind, Wood**<br>
— —

### *The Judgment*

. . . *Thou hast nothing to draw with and the well is deep* . . . (Job 4:11). The "well of water" is your subconscious mind. You can draw anything you want out of this well. The rope you use to draw up the pitcher of water is your faith and confidence in the Infinite Intelligence of your subconscious mind, the nature of which is to respond to your conviction. If you do not have the conviction, you do not make the contact.

### *The Image*

. . . *And David abode in the wood* . . . (I Samuel 23:18). Wood was used in ancient times not only for boats but also for burnt offerings. The word "David" means a man who loves or gives allegiance to the Infinite Intelligence within him, and "to abide in the wood" means that you seek sustenance, strength and wisdom from the Giver of Life within you. Wood is symbolic of the Tree of Life within you. Drink of inspiration, joy and courage.

### *The Lines*

Six at the bottom: . . . *Whosoever drinketh of this water shall thirst again. But whosoever drinketh of the water that I shall give him shall . . . be in him a well of water springing up into everlasting life* (John 4:13–14). Many do not know where the waters of life exist. The water mentioned in *I Ching* and in the Bible means the refreshing power of spiritual values. Man seeks without for security, peace and happiness; yet, these actually come from within himself. Man has impressed his subconscious mind with all kinds of false knowledge, fears and prejudice. The result is that he is governed by negative emotions, and this is called mud in Oriental symbology. Do not entertain negative emotions. Supplant them with Divine love.

Nine in the second place: . . . *Give me this water that I thirst not* . . . (John 4:15). The "well of water" refers to your inside values, your subconscious and emotional life. In this well lay all wisdom, knowledge and power. It is the infinite storehouse of all forms of immaterial life. From your subconscious are born all your experiences. You are not using the wisdom and guidance of your subconscious when you don't think right, feel right and act right. The mass mind impinges on your mind and the result is confusion, ineptitude and failure.

Nine in the third place: . . . *And he would have given thee living water* . . . (John 4:10). "Living water" means inspiration, truth, healing, guidance or whatever else you need for spiritual refreshment. You are refusing to accept the truths of your own psychological capacity to be independent and free from limitation, trouble, pain and misery. Begin to drink from the Fountain of Life within you.

Six in the fourth place: *The mouth of a righteous man is a well of life* . . . (Proverbs 10:11). As you continue to think on whatsoever things are true, lovely, and noble, you will gradually change the negative patterns in your subconscious mind. You become aware of a gradual change as you begin to think constructively based on eternal verities.

Nine in the fifth place: *Ho, every one that thirsteth, come ye to the waters . . . buy wine and milk without money and without price* (Isaiah 55:1). Begin to tune in on the Infinite within you and claim inspiration, guidance, Divine love and harmony—then you are drinking of the waters of Infinite Life, the Fountain Which never runs dry. The price you pay is attention, devotion and recognition of the Source from which all blessings flow. All things are working together for good for you now.

Six in the sixth place: *As cold waters to a thirsty soul, so is good news from a far country* (Proverbs 25:25). You are thirsty spiritually when you lack joy, peace, inspiration and confidence. Claim that the Living Spirit Almighty (Living Waters) flows through you as wisdom, truth and beauty, and as joy, harmony, power and love; you will receive countless blessings from On High. You are drawing power from the Eternal Well within you now, and everything you do will prosper in a wonderful way.

## 49. Ko/Revolution (Molting)

- -
— **above Tui, The Joyous, Lake**
—
—
- - **below Li, The Clinging, Fire**
—

*The Judgment*

*And be not conformed to this world; but be ye transformed by the renewing of your mind . . .* (Romans 12:2). By giving up all your old traditional beliefs and enthroning in your mind principles and truths of life, which are the same yesterday, today and forever, you will advance along all lines. Feed your subconscious mind with life-giving patterns, and wonders will happen in your life. The past is forgotten and remembered no more. Success is assured you.

*The Image*

*And whosoever was not found written in the book of life was cast into the lake of fire* (Revelation 20:15). The book of life is your subconscious mind and you are always writing in it your impressions, beliefs, opinions, and sundry concepts, good and bad. The lake of fire represents the fires of conscience, those searing flames of fear, guilt and hostility which torment the soul of man. You are now dissolving all these negative emotions with the soothing power of Divine love and harmony, and His river of peace floods your mind and heart, and you are bringing order and harmony into your mind, body and circumstances.

*The Lines*

Nine at the bottom: *And it shall come to pass on that day that a man shall nourish a young cow . . .* (Isaiah 7:21). The cow is a symbol of your subconscious mind, and also of that desire of yours which, when realized, would nourish you. A cow gives milk and is a symbol of nourishment, tranquility, and peace of mind. Remain quiet and peaceful for the time being, continue to nourish your ideal with faith and confidence, and you will grow stronger gradually until you reach your goal.

Six in the second place: *See, I have this day set thee over the nations . . . to root out, and to pull down, and to destroy, and to throw down, to build and to plant* (Jeremiah 1:10). This means you are to act decisively and dynamically in rooting out of your mind all false beliefs, erroneous opinions and ill will of all kinds. It also means that you must completely change your way of doing things in your home and business and affirm and do everything from the standpoint of the law of love and Divine harmony. You will then experience a real revolution in all phases of your life, you will meet all problems with faith in God, and you will overcome.

Nine in the third place: *Casting all your care upon him, for he careth for you* (I Peter 5:7). . . . *He that believeth shall not make haste* (Isaiah 28:16). In prayer the less effort you make the better. Pray quietly and peacefully. If you are in the ocean, you don't beat the waters violently to keep afloat. Turn to the Creative Intelligence within you with confidence and faith and do not waver and vacillate. Affirm that Infinite Intelligence is opening up the way for you in Divine order. Believe you are Divinely guided. Let your prayers be an unhurried communion with the Indwelling God. Remind yourself that nothing is impossible to God; expect results, and you will get results.

Nine in the fourth place: *For behold, I create new heavens and a new earth: and the former shall not be remembered, nor come into mind* (Isaiah 65:17). A "new heaven" is a mind dedicated to God and the truths of life, and then there follows automatically a new earth, meaning new conditions, circumstances and environmental changes to conform to the new mental pattern. The past is dead, and you no longer dwell on old hurts and grievances. You have now established a new government in your mind. Right action, justice, goodwill, honesty and integrity govern your mind, and many blessings follow this new government enthroned there.

Nine in the fifth place: *For I am the Lord, I change not . . .* (Malachi 3:6). The God-Presence never changes. It is the same yesterday, today and forever. As you contemplate the truths of God, you will change, because you become what you contemplate. Continue to fill your heart with Divine love, by thinking it, feeling it, and radiating it to all. As you do this, you will have the vivid realization of God's love which solves your problems and also enables you to help others and gain their cooperation.

Six in the sixth place: . . . *The leopard shall lie down with the kid . . . and a little child shall lead them* (Isaiah 11:6). The leopard in the *I Ching* and the Bible represents a limpid state, clear water, symbolizing beauty and harmony. The little child represents an awareness of the power of God in you. An awakening to the Spiritual power for the first time is called a child. Your mind under the direction of Divine guidance is changing into harmony, beauty, peace and understanding, and your emotions are being transformed along God-like ways. Continue to know that all things are working together for good to you. Adhere to the Truths of Being and good results will follow.

## 50. TING/THE CALDRON

——

— — **above Li, The Clinging, Fire**

——

——

—— **below Sun, The Gentle, Wind, Wood**

— —

### *The Judgment*

*Out of his nostrils goeth smoke as out of . . . a caldron* (Job 41:20). The caldron is another name for your deeper mind which is full of wisdom, power and love. The smoke coming out is your exaltation; the Spirit within you is God. You are inspired from On High and everything you do will prosper.

### *The Image*

. . . *the caldrons and the candlesticks* . . . (Jeremiah 52:19). It is said man is the candle of the Lord, symbolizing the fact that you are to shed your light (intelligence) in all phases of your life. Claim God is guiding you and Divine right action governs you in all ways and the caldron (your subconscious mind) will then respond, and you will find harmony and peace in your life.

### *The Lines*

Six at the bottom: . . . *This city is the caldron . . . I will bring you forth out of the midst of it* (Ezekiel 11:7). The city is your mind (caldron), and you must cleanse it regularly and systematically by giving yourself a transfusion of faith, confidence, love, joy and goodwill. As you fill your mind with these qualities, you neutralize and wipe out all negative patterns in your subconscious mind (the caldron). The lower is always subject to the higher. You are on the way to great accomplishments and achievements.

Nine in the second place: *When he giveth quietness who then can make trouble*? (Job 34:29). Join up with the God-Presence within you. Realize that no one can hurt you, as "one with God is a majority." If someone is jealous and speaks ill of you, he cannot hurt you, because you know the negative thoughts and suggestions of others have no power to create the things they suggest. Your thought is creative and your thought is on God. His peace and great success and prosperity are experienced by you.

Nine in the third place: . . . *Where is the Lord*? *And they that handle the law knew me not* . . . (Jeremiah 2:8). The Lord is the universal subjective mind, the Lordly power within you. If you do not use this power in the right way, you will get into trouble. All the wisdom, power and intelligence you need to lead a full and happy life are within you, but you are not using your God-given powers. Begin to tap your inner reservoir and claim guidance, harmony and abundance in your life. Affirm boldly, "God rains blessings from Heaven for me," and you will experience prosperity and success.

Nine in the fourth place: . . . *The law of Moses should not be broken* . . . (John 7:23). The "law of Moses" means: you are that which you contemplate. What you think and feel, you create. You must have the faith and the confidence necessary to achieve your goal. Feelings of inferiority and inadequacy attract loss and limitation to you. You must acquire self-esteem and confidence in order to succeed. Carelessness and inattention to the values of life breed failure.

Six in the fifth place: *And two golden rings shalt thou make* . . . (Exodus 30:4). Gold means power, purity, a clear sky, and fair weather, meaning a clean mental and emotional atmosphere. A ring is symbolic of love, peace and unity with God. A ring, being a circle, is also a symbol of Infinity and of God's love. In simple, everyday language, all it means is that you are now getting your conscious and subconscious mind to agree on harmony, health, peace and right action. As you adhere to this procedure, you will, by the law of attraction, get others to aid and assist you in the realization of your heart's desire.

Nine at the top: *And thou shalt make . . . two rings of gold . . .* (Exodus 28:23). Gold represents the power of God, and jade in the *I Ching* represents purity, beauty and joy. You are identified with the spiritual values of life (gold and jade), and inasmuch as you are giving attention to the eternal truths of life, you will experience success and victory along all lines.

## 51. CHEN/THE AROUSING (SHOCK, THUNDER)

**above Chen, The Arousing, Thunder**

**below Chen, The Arousing, Thunder**

### *The Judgment*

. . . *And the Lord sent thunder and rain that day* . . . (I Samuel 12:18). Thunder creates a lot of noise and sometimes gives you a sudden shock, but it is followed by rain. . . . *Behold, I will rain bread from heaven for you* . . . (Exodus 16:4). You are Divinely guided, and blessings follow.

### *The Image*

. . . *And I heard as it were the noise of thunder* . . . (Revelation 6:1). The "noise of thunder," psychologically and spiritually speaking, means the inner movement of the Spirit in you, announcing a new birth and a new beginning, whereby you will move from the unconditioned to the conditioned state. Be persistent in knowing that Divine law and order govern your life.

*The Lines*

Nine at the bottom: *The voice of thy thunder was in the heaven . . . the earth trembled and shook* (Psalms 77:18). "Heaven" is the invisible part of you—your mind. The sound of thunder in your mind indicates a big change in your life. Have no fear; everything passes away. After the storm comes the calm. Joy and blessings come to you.

Six in the second place: *Then the earth shook and trembled . . .* (II Samuel 22:8). The earth means your body, environment, business—your external world. When you feel shook up, troubled, and when you experience setbacks and losses, do not fight these conditions or experiences mentally. Instead, identify yourself mentally and spiritually with whatever you have lost, while realizing that you never lose anything except you admit the loss mentally. "Possession is nine points of the law." Symbolically, this is called climbing nine hills. Affirm as follows: "I now feel I am one with my wealth and my possessions. I accept these mentally, knowing what I claim and feel to be true will come to pass magnified and in Divine order." You will get back all that you have lost.

Six in the third place: *The earth shook, the heavens also . . .* (Psalms 68:8). The earth means manifestations, expressions—your body, home, business life, associates. All come under the term earth, or land. Even though outer things go to pieces, such as when your health breaks down or you suffer financial loss, you are not going to be afraid. Affirm boldly and mean it: "God is my refuge and my fortress. God is an ever present help. God knows and God cares. God brings about a Divine solution." Pray in this manner and you will rise above all your problems.

Nine in the fourth place: *Let God arise, let his enemies be scattered . . .* (Psalms 68:1). The enemies are fear, doubt, self-condemnation, ill will and anger. "Let God arise" means to exalt the wisdom and power of God within you, and this Presence will rise like a fountain and fall as a blessing and benediction. When your mind is muddled and confused and you indulge negative thoughts, you remain frustrated and blocked.

Six in the fifth place: *The heathen raged, the kingdoms were moved* . . . (Psalms 46:6). The heathen means your erroneous thoughts, fears, doubts, self-criticisms and negations of every kind that disturb your mind and cause you to be confused and depressed. Hold steadfastly to the God-Presence within you by contemplating harmony and Divine right action; and claim His river of peace flows through you, and the kingdom of error and turbulence will be moved. Equilibrium and serenity will be restored to you.

Six in the sixth place: *Be still, and know that I am God. I will be exalted among the heathen, I will be exalted in the earth* (Psalms 46:10). Do not rehearse grievances or fight problems in your mind. Turn resolutely away from the turbulence and confusion and contemplate God's healing love and harmony flowing through you and all your affairs. This is the way out of trouble. Remember, error and fear are always hurried; they tend to sweep you off your feet. This is the time to be still and know that God is bringing about a Divine solution. Do not let others disturb you. They are responsible for their own thinking.

## 52. KEN/KEEPING STILL, MOUNTAIN

——
— — **above Ken, Keeping Still, Mountain**
— —
——
— — **below Ken, Keeping Still, Mountain**
— —

*The Judgment*

*Be still and know that I am God . . .* (Psalms 46:10). This means that you quiet your mind and turn inward, and you know that God is God. The quiet contemplation of God is the most potent action of all. Immobilize your attention and focus on the God-Presence within you. Your eyes are closed, your body is relaxed and at ease; then meditate on the bliss, harmony, peace, power, beauty and majesty of the Infinite One. Realize God is Supreme Intelligence, Boundless Love, Absolute Harmony and Infinite Wisdom. As you do this, a river of life and love will flow through you, and you will find yourself Divinely prospered in all ways.

*The Image*

*Thy righteousness is like the great mountains . . .* (Psalms 36:6). Mountains in the *I Ching* and in the Bible mean Spiritual thought or contemplation of God. Righteousness is right thinking. Think quietly and with interest on the project at hand. Look at it from all angles and know that you are Divinely inspired to do the right thing, and that is exactly what you will do.

*The Lines*

Six at the bottom: *And as the toes of the feet were part of iron and part of clay . . .* (Daniel 2:42). "Toes of your feet" means understanding of the laws of mind. "Iron" and "clay" mean strong and weak ideas—a sort of wavering. Be still and quiet, tune in with the Infinite Intelligence, and continue in right thought, right feeling, and right action, and you will arrive at your goal.

Six in the second place: *With God nothing shall be impossible* (Luke 1:37). When trouble and difficulty seem beyond your control, put the problem in God's hands and affirm: "God will perfect that which concerneth me." Refuse to go along with anything contrary to goodness, truth, beauty and plain honesty, or you will experience regret.

Nine in the third place: *And he smote them hip and thigh . . .* (Judges 15:8). "Hip and thigh" in the *I Ching* and in the Bible refer to the sex organs and sexual desire. Repression and suppression of urges are not the answer, as these give rise to inner conflicts. All urges and desires, are to be channeled in God-like ways. The sex act should be one of love, not lust. Austerities, rigidities, postures and mental and physical gymnastics are not the way to commune with God. The real way is through the heart and through the practice of the Presence, which simply means meditating on your highest concept of God.

Six in the fourth place: *When he giveth quietness, who then can make trouble*? (Job 34:29). A good way to relax the body is to speak to your body as follows: "My toes are relaxed, calves of my legs are relaxed, my spine is completely relaxed, my heart and lungs are relaxed, my shoulders are relaxed, my neck is relaxed, my brain is relaxed, my whole body is completely relaxed. God's river of peace flows through me." As you affirm these truths, your body relaxes, as it must obey you. Your body moves as it is moved upon. Your body acts as it is acted upon. When you are relaxed and when your mind is in tune with the Infinite, the wisdom of God arises to your surface mind and you will be inspired from On High.

Six in the fifth place: *Let your speech be always with grace, seasoned with salt, that ye may know how ye ought to answer every man* (Colossians 4:6). Watch your words. Words are thoughts expressed. Salt is a preservative, but it also makes the food more palatable. Grace means the wisdom and love of God functioning through you. Let your speech be graceful, constructive and full of goodwill to all, and all regret vanishes.

Nine in the sixth place: *And into whatsoever house ye enter, first say, peace be to this house* (Luke 10:5). Quiet your mind periodically and contemplate the God of peace, and you will feel His river of peace moving over the desolate areas of your mind, refreshing, inspiring and guiding you in all ways. Having found this inner peace through the stilling of your mind and putting it in tune with the Infinite, you will give the benediction of peace to all who come within your orbit. Blessings and prosperity are assured you.

## 53. CHIEN/DEVELOPMENT (GRADUAL PROGRESS)

——
—— **above Sun, The Gentle, Wind, Wood**
— —
——
— — **below Ken, Keeping Still, Mountain**
— —

*The Judgment*

*So then he that giveth her in marriage doeth well . . .* (I Corinthians 7:38). Marriage in the *I Ching* and in the Bible has more than one meaning. You marry your idea, desire or aspiration by uniting with it mentally and emotionally and remaining faithful every step of the way, knowing that the power and wisdom of your subconscious will bring it to pass. It is somewhat like courting a girl. You praise her, exalt her, woo her with gifts and attention, and if you remain faithful to her, the courting process culminates in marriage, and the two become one. In the prayer procedure, the same process takes place. Be faithful to the end.

*The Image*

*. . . To him that overcometh will I give to eat of the tree of life . . .* (Revelation 2:7). You eat of the tree of life when you meditate or mentally feast on that which is elevating, dignifying and praiseworthy. The tree of life is the Presence of God within you. Everything you are seeking is within you. As you feast on harmony, peace, joy, and love and radiate these qualities to others, your whole world will change and you will experience progressively more harmonious relationships with others.

*The Lines*

Six at the bottom . *In quietness and in confidence shall be your strength* . (Isaiah 30:15). Realization of your goal, objective or heart's desire doesn't always come in one move, but usually in a series of stages. These intermediate stages or steps should be welcomed. You may meet with temporary delays, setbacks or criticism, but you should merely regard these passing irritations as stepping-stones to your progress. Continue praying for the next higher step and you will move ahead.

Six in the second place: . . . *Nothing shall by any means hurt you* (Luke 10:19). You are on the way, and you feel secure because of your sense of oneness with the Infinite within you. If you were in Oakland on the way to San Francisco and you were on the San Francisco Bridge, you would be on your way to your destination. Every improvement and advancement is a movement toward your heart's desire. Success and prosperity are yours.

Nine in the third place: *Acquaint now thyself with Him and be at peace* (Job 22:21). Don't hurry. Haste makes waste of energy, vitality and discernment. Don't resent or condemn yourself or others. Rise up in consciousness and set yourself and others free. Forgiveness is the best medicine. Trying to force things, using mental coercion, blocks your good and brings loss to you. Tune in on the God-Presence. Feel God's peace and power. Think good and good will follow.

Six in the fourth place: *Casting all your care upon him, for he careth for you* (I Peter 5:7). When you are troubled, worried or in danger, surrender to the God-Presence within you. Cling steadfastly to the truth that there is an answer for every prayer, peace for seeming discord, and protection from all harm. You will be protected.

Nine in the fifth place: *A talebearer revealeth secrets; but he that is of a faithful spirit concealeth the matter* (Proverbs 11:13). As you move upward in life and put your head above the crowd, people throw stones at you, i.e., they may gossip about you and show jealousy. If you permit others to hurt you or disturb you emotionally, you hinder your own development. Bless them and walk on. You will go where your vision is, and you will experience harmony and promotion.

Nine at the top: *How beautiful upon the mountains are the feet of him that bringeth good tidings, that publisheth peace, that bringeth good tidings of good* . . . (Isaiah 52:7). You carry happiness and glad tidings about within you. The peace of God reigns in your heart and the light of God shines in you. Your journey is onward, upward and Godward.

## 54. KUEI MEI/THE MARRYING MAIDEN

— —

— — **above Chen, The Arousing, Thunder**

———

— —

——— **below Tui, The Joyous, Lake**

———

*The Judgment*

. . . *The children of this world marry and are given in marriage* (Luke 20:34). Your "marriage" is your conception or estimate of yourself, and your "children" represent the experiences, conditions and events of your life based on your inner feeling about yourself. Your receptive attitude of mind while praying can be likened to a maiden or a bride or a womb, for it receives impressions. The dominant idea you have is the husband, for it is that which impregnates the subconscious, or the maiden. You must unite with the highest and the best. Do not demean or belittle yourself or indulge in mediocrity or inferiority. If you do, the results will be failure and limitation of all kinds.

*The Image*

. . . *What therefore God hath joined together, let not man put asunder* (Matthew 19:6). God is love, and when true love in the heart unites a man and a woman together, that is God joining a couple in a sacred covenant. When difficulties and arguments arise, each one dissolves the problem in the light of God's love. Each remains faithful to the marriage vow, and inasmuch as there is a true spiritual union between two people, there is no divorce, for none is wanted. Love, goodwill and understanding are the keys to all human relations.

*The Lines*

Nine at the bottom: *Who then is that faithful and wise steward, whom his lord shall make ruler over his household . . .* (Luke 12:42). We are all stewards working in the vineyards of our minds. When you do your job joyously and faithfully, you will find that your subconscious (the Lord) responds and promotes you and removes obstacles. Have a constructive vision, be faithful to your vision, show respect for authority; then the reaction of the law (your subconscious) will be constructive and prosper you along all lines.

Nine in the second place: . . . *If therefore thine eye be single, thy whole body shall be full of light* (Matthew 6:22). The eye symbolizes spiritual perception. Whatever you give attention to is that which controls and directs your life. Regardless of what others have done to you—whether they have been unfaithful or have betrayed your trust—steadfastly direct your attention to God, the Living Spirit within you. When you contemplate the glory of God and His peace, and when God comes first into your life, then the law of God (your subconscious) will respond and your whole embodiment and experiences will be good.

Six in the third place: . . . *No good thing will he withhold from them that walk uprightly* (Psalms 84:11). Stop thinking you have to compromise with life. You have the capacity to go within and claim your good, and your subconscious will respond and validate your claim. God is the giver and the gift, and you must claim that which was given to you. God indwells you and is the very life of you. Raise your sights and remember that you go where your vision is. Cease demeaning and demoting yourself. Exalt God in the midst of you, mighty to do all things for you.

Nine in the fourth place: . . . *to be spiritually minded is life and peace* (Romans 8:6). Premarital sexual experiences are not conducive to a happy married life. Often, the man distrusts the woman he can have so easily. He says to himself, "If she will do this before marriage, she will do it with others afterwards." Happiness in marriage depends on love, loyalty, honesty, a devotion to the truth, and a desire to lift up each other spiritually, mentally and in all ways. Love does not take a woman to a shabby motel; neither is love expressed furtively by an illicit interlude in a parked car. Loyalty and purity pay great dividends, and you experience the joy of the answered prayer.

Six in the fifth place: *Let nothing be done through strife or vainglory, but in lowliness of mind . . . look not every man on his own things, but every man also on the things of others* (Philippians 2:3–4). You are free from pretension and not blinded by self-conceit. With understanding comes humility, and you do all for the glory of God, and great blessings come to you.

Six in the sixth place: *And thou shalt put them into one basket . . .* (Exodus 29:3). The basket means your heart, your subconscious mind, from which all experiences come. The fruits that should come forth are love, joy, peace, gentleness, faith, confidence and goodwill. When you pray, your conscious mind and your subconscious must agree and synchronize. The mind and the heart must unite. There must be feeling, animation and enthusiasm before you can bring forth good fruit such as health, happiness, abundance and security. Intellectual assent or verbalism without incorporating the truths in your heart accomplishes nothing.

## 55. Feng/Abundance (Fullness)

— —<br>
— — **above Chen, The Arousing, Thunder**<br>
——<br>
——<br>
— — **below Li, The Clinging, Flame**<br>
——

*The Judgment*

*For whosoever hath, to him shall be given, and he shall have more abundance* . . . (Matthew 13:12). When you walk in the consciousness of God's abundance, realizing that God is the Source of all blessings, and when you give allegiance and loyalty to the real Source, your subconscious magnifies and multiplies your good exceedingly. Be like the sun at midday. It casts no shadows, meaning that nothing must deflect you from your aim, which is to express more of God's life, love, truth, beauty and prosperity.

*The Image*

*But the meek shall inherit the earth; and shall delight themselves in the abundance of peace* (Psalms 37:11). The meek are those people who are open and receptive to the Truth of Being. They look at no man as their enemy, as they know all enemies are in their own minds, such as fear, ignorance, superstition, doubt and ill will. The meek feel a oneness with God, the Source of all blessings, and give no power to others or to conditions. While all men may not be their friends, they also are not their enemies. They realize that one with God is a majority, and having established peace of mind within themselves, all good things are added to them.

*The Lines*

Nine at the bottom: . . . *for of the abundance of the heart his mouth speaketh* (Luke 6:45). The "heart" is your subconscious mind, and inasmuch as you have impressed your subconscious with the idea of wealth, prosperity and success, you will attract the right person who cooperates with you in Divine order. Your speech and all your actions indicate your awareness of God's abundance.

Six in the second place: . . . *Suddenly are my tents spoiled, and my curtains in a moment* (Jeremiah 4:20). You are the tent or the tabernacle of the Living God, and your curtain is your mind which conceals your thoughts, feelings and beliefs. Do not permit envy or jealousy of others to deflect you from your goal. Give no power to others, but give all power and recognition to God within you, realizing if God be for you, who can be against you? Resist not evil, but overcome evil with good thoughts and faith and confidence in the Almighty Power Which responds to you and leads you to victory and the fulfillment of your heart's desire. Success is yours.

Nine in the third place: . . . *The sun became black as sackcloth of hair* . . . (Revelation 6:12). One of the meanings of the sun in the *I Ching* and in the Bible is your conscious mind. The moon is called the subconscious. The moon shines by reflection of the sun; likewise, your subconscious mind is always reflecting your habitual thinking. Blackness means darkness, confusion, intrigue. When you are beset with what seem to be insurmountable obstacles and difficulties, sit still; don't advance. Sit steady in the boat and let things take their course, trusting in the Divine law to adjust all things.

Nine in the fourth place: . . . *The Lord my God will enlighten my darkness* (Proverbs 18:28). Darkness means difficulties, ignorance and fear. Light dispels the darkness. Realize that Infinite Intelligence within your subconscious mind knows the way out and reveals to you the answer. You are Divinely guided, and the Guiding Principle within you attracts to you those who aid you in the realization of your dream. The day breaks for you and all the shadows flee away. Success is yours.

Six in the fifth place: *But my God shall supply all your need according to his riches in glory* . . . (Philippians 4:19). Your deeper mind magnifies and multiplies your good exceedingly, and you are Divinely guided in all ways and will automatically attract the right people who cooperate, aid and assist you. Many blessings are yours now.

Six in the sixth place: *And I will say to my soul, Soul, thou hast much goods laid up for many years . . . But God said unto him, Thou fool, this night thy soul shall be required of thee: then whose shall those things be, which thou hast provided*? (Luke 12:19,20). Wealth and possessions are not a deterrent to spirituality. All these things are necessary on this three-dimensional plane. Remember you do not really possess anything. God possesses all. You are a steward of the Divine and should use your wealth and possessions wisely, judiciously and constructively. You should share wisely with your family and contribute to the common good, while claiming that the wisdom of God guides you in all your actions. When you go on to the next dimension, the only things you can take with you are the treasures in your mind, which should include wisdom, love, faith, confidence, generosity and reverence for the Divinity which is the Source of yourself and all blessings. You owe your success also to others who helped you on the way. Love unites you with your family and all men. The really rich man is the man who recognizes the Source of all good. He is always rich in wisdom, understanding, kindness, love and goodwill to all. Looking down on others, having a superiority complex, and being smug and complacent attract loss to you in many ways.

## 56. LU/THE WANDERER

——
— — **above Li, The Clinging, Fire**
——
——
— — **below Ken, Keeping Still, Mountain**
— —

*The Judgment*

*He wandereth abroad for bread, saying, where is it?* . . . (Job 15:23). When you travel throughout this world, regardless of the state or country, realize that the real bread of life is the Presence of God within you. Sense that God is guiding you and that the All-Powerful One and the All-Wise One is taking care of you and that He supplies all your needs and guides you in your footsteps so that you make no errors. No one can assimilate or digest good for another. Let your contact with God be a living one. Radiate love and goodwill to all and you will prosper and succeed in your journeys.

*The Image*

*As a bird that wandereth from her nest, so is a man that wandereth from his place* (Proverbs 27:8). Your place is always to be one with God and to realize as you sense this union that Divine law and order govern you in all ways. Come to quick decisions on what is right and just and do not deviate from the principle of right action. Come back to the nest, which means come back to the center of your own being where God dwells and insists on honesty, integrity and fortune for yourself and all those concerned.

*The Lines*

Six at the bottom: . . . *Wandering about from house to house . . . busybodies, speaking things which they ought not* (I Timothy 5:13). The Bible says: *And in whatsoever house ye enter, first say, peace be to this house* (Luke 10:5). Let the benediction be in your heart whenever you come into the presence of another or enter his home. Do not engage in negative speech or condemnation of others. Let your speech be constructive, wholesome and uplifting. Criticizing others and holding them up to ridicule bring loss and limitation to yourself.

Six in the second place: *With my whole heart have I sought thee: O let me not wander from thy commandments* (Psalms 119:10). The chief commandment is to love the God-Presence, which means to give the Presence your supreme allegiance and devotion and to keep in tune with the Infinite. As you love, respect and honor the Higher Self of you which is God, you will automatically respect and honor the Divinity in others, thereby gaining the cooperation of men and women and attracting the right companion for you through life.

Nine in the third place: . . . *There was no room for them at the inn* (Luke 2:7). The inn is where men gather to gossip and find fault, and where the mass mind governs with its superstitions, fears, hates, anger and hostilities. There is no room in such a mind for a realization of the Divine Presence which can heal, restore your mind to peace, and guide and direct you. God is the great stranger to millions of people. When you think your intellect and your ego can solve the problems of life and when you fail to contact Infinite Intelligence and be governed by Its power and wisdom, you get into trouble and attract loss.

Nine in the fourth place: *Look unto me and be ye saved, all the ends of the earth* . . .(Isaiah 45:22). To dwell upon negative things such as insecurity, personal danger and feeling alienated from others will only cause the manufacture of more trouble. Realize that God loves you and cares for you, and that you are always secure when you dwell consciously on the truth that you abide under the shadow of the Almighty. This is your refuge and your fortress and your true home. Failure to make contact with the Infinite causes you to feel like a stranger in a strange land.

Six in the fifth place: . . . *God is love; and he that dwelleth in love dwelleth in God, and God in him* (I John 4:16). Love or goodwill to others is always creative. A sense of love lengthens your life, brings inspiration, opens new doors for you, attracts new friends, expands your interests and business and overcomes all obstacles. With a heart full of love for all, you are always welcome everywhere and you cease being a stranger.

Nine at the sixth place: . . . *as a wandering bird cast out of the nest* . . . (Isaiah 16:2). You are the nest where God dwells, and when you take care of the nest, which is your mind and body, God will take care of you. You must not permit the fires of anger, resentment and hostility to burn up that nest. The cow in the *I Ching* and the Bible represents the milk of human kindness, love, peace and simplicity. When you fail to practice and identify with these qualities, you attract loss and limitation.

## 57. SUN/THE GENTLE (THE PENETRATING, WIND)

——
—— **above Sun, The Gentle, Wind, Wood**
— —
——
—— **below Sun, The Gentle, Wind, Wood**
— —

*The Judgment*

*And the servant of the Lord must not strive; but be gentle unto all men* . . . (II Timothy 2:24). Do not be impatient with yourself. Despise not the day of small beginnings. Handle yourself as a wise parent handles a difficult or obstreperous child—kindly, patiently, but with gentle firmness, not expecting immediate growth, though nevertheless realizing and knowing that growth and expansion is on the way. Keep your eyes on your goal, be a good servant of the law, which means that whatever you steadfastly behold and on which you focus your attention grows inevitably and comes to pass. Know that God is guiding you and move forward in your plans with confidence. Take advice also from a good counselor.

*The, Image*

*The wind bloweth where it listeth . . .* (John 3:8). The wind is symbolic of the Spirit within you. Open your mind and heart to the influx of the Spirit. Claim that the Spirit of God is flowing through your thoughts, words and deeds. This mental work is invisible, silent and gentle. It is the most far-reaching activity in your life and is subconsciously received and experienced by all those around you. Build your temple (your personality) without noise—your thought is soundless. Think good and good follows along all lines.

*The Lines*

Six at the bottom: . . . *Faith without works is dead* (James 2:20). Oftentimes as we pray, we notice that for a long time there seems to be no change in our outer world, but if we persist and keep our faith strong and cease vacillating and wavering, in spite of appearances, the way will open up. We must keep our faith in God and all things good, and good results will come to pass.

Nine in the second place: . . . *God is light, and in him is no darkness at all* (I John 1:5). God is love and Intelligence—All-Powerful. Hold up your fearful thoughts or sense of guilt to the light of your own reason and you will realize these are thoughts in your own mind which have no reality or power behind them. Negative suggestions given you have no power except you accept them, and then it is a movement solely of your own thought. Let the Light of God shine in your mind and realize that predictions of evil or harm have no power except you accept them. Keep your faith in God and realize as you tune in with the Infinite and claim Divine law and order in your life, all your ways will be roads of pleasantness and all your paths will be peaceful. There is no power to challenge God. One with God is a majority. Great blessings are yours.

Nine in the third place: . . . *In quietness and in confidence shall be your strength* . . . (Isaiah 30:15). Avoid picking and nagging at your problems from time to time all day long. This mental attitude prolongs your problem. Look over the situation from all angles, claim God is guiding you, and then come at once to a clear-cut, definite decision, while knowing that the subjective wisdom of your subconscious will respond in Divine order. If you vacillate and waver, the result will be confusion and frustration.

Six in the fourth place: *And ye shall seek me, and find me, when ye shall search for me with all your heart* (Jeremiah 29:13). Realize that right thinking and the practice of the Presence of God, which is harmony, health, peace, wholeness and abundance, follows an unbreakable law and leads you to the fulfillment of your goal. Put your heart into your goal, which means let love and enthusiasm into your project, and you will find the answer.

Nine in the fifth place: . . . *Be not faithless, but believing* (John 20:27). Have faith in your own faith. Be determined in your own mind that you really have faith in the Guiding Principle within you. If you have no faith, you will not pray. The mere fact that you are praying means you have enough faith with which to start. Continue trusting the Infinite Intelligence within your subconscious to guide and direct you in all ways. Many blessings are yours.

Nine at the top: *Oh foolish Galatians, who hath bewitched you?* (Galatians 3:1). You bewitch yourself when you think wrongly, thus you build up false conditions around you and you believe them to be real. You forget you are the cause. You are bewitched by negative thoughts and emotions. Know that God is All Power, Infinite Intelligence and Boundless Love. If you refuse to call upon this Presence and Power and choose to indulge in negativity, losses come into your experience.

## 58. Tui/The Joyous, Lake

— —
—— **above Tui, The Joyous, Lake**
——
— —
—— **below Tui, The Joyous, Lake**
——

*The Judgment*

. . . *In thy presence is fullness of joy* . . . (Psalms 16:11). Take a source of keen delight and pleasure in your work or profession. Display a glad feeling, and this mood will be felt also by others. Great delight comes to you when you know that your thought is creative. Therefore, when you think of whatsoever things are lovely, noble and God-like, you are assured that the Living Spirit will flow through the forces of your thought patterns, bringing all your good to pass. No one can take away this knowledge from you. This is the joy of the Lord (Law) which gives you strength in all your undertakings. When you pray (think) realize it is a joyous visit with God within you. Practice this and your world will change in a wonderful way.

*The Image*

. . . *At thy right hand there are pleasures for evermore* (Psalms 16:11). The word "hand" in the *I Ching* and in the Bible means the Power of God, and the "right hand" means using the Power wisely and constructively. Spirit is God and is the Supreme Power and Cause. Feel and know that the Spirit of God is flowing through your thoughts and imagery, and as you begin with joy, you will end in triumph and success. The beginning and the end are the same. To know this is to give you joy. Joy is felicity, gladness of the heart; it is laughter, goodwill, harmony and peace. The Bible says: *A merry heart doeth good like a medicine* . . . (Proverbs 17:22). This attitude instills joy and satisfaction in all those around you.

*The Lines*

Nine at the bottom: . . . *And shout for joy, all ye that are upright in heart* (Psalms 32:11). Recently an engineer told me that he had a most difficult assignment and had experienced many failures in the project; but he said that he endured burning the midnight oil and the travail of many setbacks and disappointments, for the joy that was set before him—the joy of victory and overcoming. He triumphed, which gave him a radiant feeling of joy. This is the way for you to approach life, and then you will be blessed and possess the power to overcome all difficulties.

Nine in the second place: *A man hath joy by the answer of his mouth: and a word spoken in due season, how good is it* (Proverbs 15:23). Your words of encouragement and confidence to others can lift them up and also give you an inner joy to see them grow and expand. Everything you do and say should give you joy and happiness. Your joy and strength and prosperity consist in practicing the Presence of God in your home, your office and everywhere else in your environment. Your inner joy comes from contact with the Infinite within you, and you find wonders happening in your life.

Six in the third place: *Folly is joy to him that is destitute of wisdom* . . . (Proverbs 15:21). Are you looking for joy in externals such as silly plays, jungle music, cheap radio and television plays or in salacious drama and other similar kinds of synthetic entertainment? If so, all this leads to frustration. *The joy of the Lord is your strength* (Nehemiah 8:10).

Nine in the fourth place: *Thou wilt keep him in perfect peace, whose mind is stayed on thee; because he trusteth in thee* (Isaiah 26:3). You must come to a decision. The right decision is to focus your attention on eternal truths of life. Your real joy comes from getting acquainted with the spiritual powers within you. Spirit within you is God—the Cause of all. Look upon It as your lord and master.

It is Omnipotent and Supreme. Join up with this Power in your thought and realize Divine love flows through you and all your thoughts and mental images, and also goes before you making joyous and happy your way. This attitude stirs up an inner joy in you. It is called worship of God, which means recognizing and devoting your attention to the Supreme Being and the Power and Cause in you and singing the song of triumph. Come to the right decision now and the joy of the Lord will be your strength.

Nine in the fifth place . . . *In quietness and in confidence shall be your strength* . . . (Isaiah 30:15). Your confidence should not be placed on externals, conditions and circumstances. All these things pass away. Quiet your mind, relax, let go mentally, and turn your attention to the God-Presence within, which never changes and which is absolutely dependable—the same yesterday, today and forever. Your real faith should be in God and in all things good and not in the transitory and ephemeral things of life.

Six in the sixth place: *Go thy way, eat thy bread with joy* . . . (Ecclesiastes 9:7). There is a spiritual food you must eat if you want to experience real joy in life. Joy consists of the practice of the Presence of God. Mentally eat of harmony, right action, peace, love, goodwill and inspiration from On High. Busy your mind with these things and joy will be yours. If you are carried away by the blandishments and enticements of the world, and your attitude is one of eat, drink and be merry, and if you are governed by sensual pleasures only, then you will be governed by the mass mind, which results in failure and frustration. By refusing to govern yourself with God's ideas, you will become a victim of the fears and limitations of the mass mind and subject to the vagaries of every wind that blows.

## 59. Huan/Dispersion (Dissolution)

———

——— **above Sun, The Gentle, Wind**

— —

— —

——— **below K'an, The Abysmal, Water**

— —

### *The Judgment*

*The lips of the wise disperse knowledge* . . . (Proverbs 15:7). You are wise when you become acquainted with the laws of life and the way of the Spirit within you. The Life-Principle is the common progenitor of all men. All of us have one Father, and we are all intimately related. Love, harmony and goodwill unite people regardless of race, creed or color. You can pour forth love, peace and goodwill to all, and you can help disseminate knowledge of the great principles of life which never change and which belong to all men. It is to your advantage to move toward your goal. Your motives being God-like, you will reach your goal, and whatever journey you take will be in Divine order.

### *The Image*

*Let thy fountains be dispersed abroad* . . . (Proverbs 5:16). The Fountain of Life is within you. Drink of the waters of inspiration, guidance, assurance and confidence As you call upon this Supreme Power and Presence, It responds to you, and you feel refreshed and exhilarated. Wish for everyone what you wish for yourself. Recognizing the Source and knowing your capacity to go within and claim what you want dispenses with all greed, envy and jealousy. The Fountain of Life responds to all who call upon It and who believe in its responsive nature.

*The Lines*

Six at the bottom: *The horse is prepared against the day of battle* . . . (Proverbs 21:31). The horse represents your emotional forces. These forces must always be channeled in God-like ways. Focus your attention on harmony, Divine right action and Divine understanding. Realize that Divine understanding and Divine love in you dissolve all misunderstandings. As you become aware that Divine love goes before you in all your undertakings, your emotional nature will flow in response and you will experience prosperity and success.

Nine in the second place: *And when ye stand praying, forgive, if ye have ought against any* . . . (Mark 11:25). To forgive is to "give for." Give yourself the mood of love, peace and goodwill for any feeling of ill will, hatred or resentment you may hold toward another. You are the only thinker in your world, and what you think and feel about another, you create in your own experience. Resentment and ill will block your good. Surrender others to God and wish for them all the blessings of life. You know when you have forgiven, because you no longer have any sting. Forgive and go free.

Six in the third place: *Seek ye first the Kingdom of God* . . . (Matthew 6:33). Set your mind on the limitless Power which is within you. Be patient and rest assured that the Spirit in you leads, guides and directs all your actions. Contemplate the reality of your goal or objective and know that an Almighty Power is moving on your behalf and will lead you to attain your objectives in Divine order.

Six in the fourth place: *The way of the Lord is strength to the upright* . . . (Proverbs 10:29). *Blessed is the man whose strength is in Thee* (Psalms 84:5). Everything that you do must be done from the standpoint of eternal truths and principles of life. All those around you should be spiritual links in the chain of your growth, welfare and prosperity and also for the common good. You should sever all connections with those who deviate from the principles of honesty, integrity and justice and adhere instead to the Truth of Being, which never changes. As you do this, great blessings and success will be experienced by you.

Nine in the fifth place: *Doth not wisdom cry? and understanding put forth her voice?* (Proverbs 8:1). Wisdom is the awareness of the

Presence and Power of God in you Which can solve all problems and bring peace to the troubled mind. Understanding is the application of this wisdom in your daily life to rise above all barriers, obstacles and difficulties. Whenever you seem to be stymied or blocked, remember there is always an answer, a solution, and that the God-Presence knows only the answer. Affirm: "God knows the way out and reveals to me the answer, and I follow the *lead* which comes to me." An idea will well up from your subliminal depths which solves your problem.

Nine at the top: *There shall no evil befall thee, neither shall any plague come nigh thy dwelling* (Psalms 91:10). You believe the God-Power is your refuge and fortress, and by dwelling regularly on the truth that God's love surrounds you and all members of your family, no trouble can touch you. Meditating regularly on the guidance and protection of God and walking and acting under that assumption, you become immune from any kind of danger. Right action prevails for you.

## 60. CHIEH/LIMITATION

— —
——— **above K'an, The Abysmal, Water**
— —
— —
——— **below Tui, The Joyous, Lake**
———

*The Judgment*

. . . *And of thy mercies toward me? Are they restrained?* (Isaiah 63:15). God is limitless, but man is limited. It is through your limitations that you discover your Divinity and the powers within you which enable you to sharpen your mental and spiritual tools and rise above all problems. Rest and motion are necessary also, as these are the great laws of life. You require a certain amount of recreation, relaxation, joy and merriment—not too much, just enough. You require time for prayer, meditation, and rest and sleep, also. Both are essential to a balanced life. In other words, moderation is required in all things. Remember, however, that the God-Power in you is not limited in any way, and that your union with It can cause you to rise and transcend your difficulties. Avoid extremes. Nature abhors extremes.

*The Image*

*For with God nothing shall be impossible* (Luke 1:37). If any problem or difficulty seems beyond your control, come to a decision in your mind that the challenge or difficulty is Divinely outmatched, and look upon it as an opportunity for growth and spiritual advancement. Affirm boldly: "God will perfect that which concerneth me." Tremendous power lies back of this truth.

*The Lines*

Nine at the bottom: *Discretion shall preserve thee, understanding shall keep thee* (Proverbs 2:11). You have the power or right to decide or act according to your own judgment. You have freedom of choice; therefore, you are judicious and you exercise prudence in your speech and action. To live through understanding is to swim with the tide. You will not need to "battle" or swim against the king wave. Wait and pray and the right time will come; then you will know what to do and how to do it.

Nine in the second place: . . . *For he that wavereth is like a wave of the sea driven with the wind and tossed* (James 1:6). When the opportunity knocks at your door, seize it at once and move forward. When you vacillate and waver, you are like the double-minded man, unstable in all your ways. A man who is pressing up and down at the same time on an elevator doesn't go up or down. This attitude of mind attracts to you loss, disappointment and frustration.

Six in the third place: . . . *And a false balance is not good* (Proverbs 20:23). You must lead a balanced life. You are living in both a subjective and an objective world. If you devote all your time to externals, dissipating your energy unwisely and abusing your body, you will have an adverse reaction. You must nourish your mind with celestial food and meditate frequently on ideas which heal, bless, inspire, elevate and dignify your whole being. The inside controls the outside. Love and felicity in the heart will govern your external life and both will be balanced. To ignore your Divine nature and overindulge in the pleasures of the flesh will cause you to have negative results.

Six in the fourth place: . . . *For I have learned, in whatever state I am, therewith to be content* (Philippians 4:11). Have the wisdom to put up with those things you can't change. Don't dissipate your energy in trying to change the world. Remember, there is no one to change but yourself. There are a lot of things you can't change in this world, such as the rotation of the earth on its axis and the movement of the heavenly bodies. You can change yourself, however, by changing your mind and aligning yourself with the Infinite Wisdom and Infinite Power, which leads you to success and achievement.

Nine in the fifth place: . . . *Godliness is profitable unto all things* . . . (I Timothy 4:8). Let all your undertakings and adventures be God-like. Do all things for the glory of God. Wish for others what you wish for yourself. Never hold limiting or restrictive thoughts about others, as whatever you think about others you create in your own experience. Be forthright and honest and affirm that God's guidance and Divine right action govern you, and for that reason you will be exalted and prospered in all ways.

Six in the sixth place: . . . *Therefore glorify God in your body* (I Corinthians 6:20). It is wrong to abuse your body. It is an instrument of the Divine Presence. Austerities, rigidities and the ascetic life have no spiritual significance and are usually destructive to the health and harmony of the body. Your body is the nest where God dwells and you should make it a channel for vitality, wholeness, beauty and perfection. Remorse over the past is destructive, and maintaining a deep and painful regret for some wrongdoing in the past is a mental poison, which debilitates the entire organism. God never punishes. You are punishing yourself. Forgive yourself and change your habits of thinking. Change your present thinking along God-like ways, and the future will be your present thoughts made manifest. Cease your self-punishment or you will continue to experience negative reactions. Cease all self-condemnation now and exalt God in the midst of you.

## 61. CHUNG FU/INNER TRUTH

———
——— **above Sun, The Gentle, Wind**
— —
— —
——— **below Tui, The Joyous, Lake**
———

### *The Judgment*

*There shall no evil happen to the just* (Proverbs 12:21). . . . *The people that do know their God shall be strong* . . . (Daniel 11:32). You are righteous when you think right, feel right, do right and act right according to the Golden Rule and the Law of Love. Have a firm conviction in God's Love and in the goodness of God, and you will communicate this inner assumption subconsciously to others, revealing to you that all real union with others is based on the bond of love and right action. This attitude blesses you, enabling you to go forward to your goal. You will prosper.

### *The Image*

*Judge not according to appearances, but judge righteous judgment* (John 7:24). Your judgment or decision should always be based on the truth. You separate the false from the true, and you come to a decision based on the principles and truths of God, which never change. Thinking, speaking and acting from the standpoint of God's Laws, you are exercising righteous judgment.

*The Lines*

Nine at the bottom: . . .*Thy faith hath saved thee; go in peace* (Luke 7:50). Faith is confidence in spiritual principles. This is the nighest degree of confidence. Place your reliance and trust in your own inner nature, which is God in you. If your confidence is placed in externals, such as on people, stocks, bonds, or personal relationships, remember all these objects continue to change and are not stable. When you place your faith in God and the goodness of God, you will prosper and succeed.

Nine in the second place: . . . *The crane . . . observe the time of their coming* (Jeremiah 8:7). The root of the word "crane" in the *I Ching* and in the Bible is joy. When you are bubbling over with joy and enthusiasm, you automatically exude a vibration which is subjectively felt by others, and you attract to yourself spiritual companions on life's journey. Your mood has its affinities. As you walk in the consciousness of the joy of the Lord, which is your strength, your mental broadcast blesses all whose mental antennae are open to receive it. Your inner joy and uplifted state of mind are contagious, and all are blessed because you walked this way.

Six in the third place: *Thou wilt keep him in perfect peace, whose mind is stayed on thee . . .* (Isaiah 26:3). Tune in on the Infinite, which lies stretched in smiling repose within you. Claim God's river of peace flows through your thoughts, words, actions and reactions. In your relationships with people, do not be possessive or try to make them do what you think they should do, or act the way you think they should act. Never permit others to rob you of your peace of mind. Your peace and inner equilibrium and joy come from God, and not from other people. Bless them and walk on in peace.

Six in the fourth place. . . . *The sun stood still and the moon stayed* . . . (Joshua 10:13). The sun is the conscious mind and the moon represents your subconscious mind. As the moon reflects the light of the sun, so does your subconscious mind reflect the decrees or the habitual thinking and imagery of your conscious mind. When you still and quiet your conscious mind (the sun stood still) and contemplate the Presence of God's Light, Love, Truth, Power and Beauty, your subconscious is also stilled, and any of its negative movements are neutralized and stilled. When you are filled full of the feeling of being what you love to be, this is called the full moon; i.e., you have succeeded in impregnating your subconscious mind. Realize that Infinite Intelligence is guiding and directing you. Adhere to this Truth and give no power to people, and you will succeed.

Nine in the fifth place: . . . *There is no power but of God; the powers that be are ordained of God* (Romans 13:1). As you continue to recognize that God is the only Presence and Power and you feel your oneness with God, you will radiate your inner conviction to all those connected with you, and they will pick it up subjectively. All things will work together for good for you.

Nine in the sixth place: . . . *While he yet spake, the cock crew* (Luke 22:60). The cock crows at dawn, and it is said that the cock believes it creates daylight. There is no use boasting and pretending to be what you do not feel to be true in your heart. Verbalism and vain repetitions or affirmations or saying prayers by rote will avail you nothing. The truths of God must be assimilated, appropriated and digested into your mentality in the same way as a piece of bread, when digested, becomes your bloodstream. To engage in idle day-dreaming or vain repetitions will only tend to demote and demean you along all lines.

## 62. Hsiao Kuo/Preponderance of the Small

— —
— — **above Chen, The Arousing, Thunder**
———
———
— — **below Ken, Keeping Still, Mountain**
— —

*The Judgment*

. . . *For a bird of the air shall carry the voice, and that which hath wings shall tell the matter* (Ecclesiastes 10:20). A "bird" in the *I Ching* and in the Bible represents your thought and feeling. That is why it has two wings. The bird flies off into the air, but it comes down to earth for food, to build its nest and to care for its young. If you build castles in the air, you must make sure you build foundations under them so that they become a reality. Select the next reasonable step in your career—that which you feel you could accomplish—and then know that through the power of God you will succeed. When your prayer is answered, you can start up the next rung of the ladder. Be like the bird. Come back to earth. Make sure that your idea is felt as true in your heart, because any desire, plan, dream or aspiration that you nourish, sustain and emotionalize will be subjectified and come to pass. Great success is yours.

*The Image*

Focus your attention on spiritual principles and feel the River of Peace flowing through you. As your soul is filled with peace, you will radiate peace, and others will receive it intuitively. For example: If you have lost a loved one, you will rejoice in the loved one's graduation to a higher dimension of life and radiate God's love and peace to your loved one or friend. When your heart is full of peace, you will have all the money you need and will spend it freely, knowing the Source is eternal. True peace of mind brings about a regeneration, enabling you to lead a full and happy life. Avoid extremes of all kinds, and experience the peace that passeth understanding.

*The Lines*

Six at the bottom: . . . *As a bird hasteth to the snare, and knoweth not that it is for his life* (Proverbs 7:23). Recently a man of seventy was trying to keep up with his son of twenty years in handball, tennis and hiking. He was boasting of his youth and his endurance and tried to run as fast as his boy. He suffered a heart attack, however. A man of sixty or seventy should engage his mind in spiritual and mental athletics and exercise, and release the joy of the Lord which is his strength. Be your age and realize age is not the flight of years but the dawn of wisdom. If you try to force things, use mental coercion, and in general try too hard, you will not succeed.

Six in the second place: *But I will for their sakes remember the covenant of their ancestors* . . . (Leviticus 26:45). The covenant is an agreement between God and man. The Presence of God is within you, and you are God's son or expression. When you call on Infinite Intelligence, you receive a response. This truth applies to all men, as God is no respecter of persons, and neither is the law of mind. You do not pray to your ancestors. The ancestors in the *I Ching* mean your subconscious mind, which is the storehouse of wisdom and is one with Infinite Intelligence and boundless wisdom. *If any of you lack wisdom, let him ask of God, that giveth to all men liberally* . . . (James 1:5). Claim that the wisdom of God governs all your actions and predicate all actions on the truth that Infinite Intelligence is guiding and directing you, and you will then advance in Divine order.

Nine in the third place: *Thou shalt not be afraid for the terror by night; nor for the arrow that flieth by day* (Psalms 91:5) The "arrow . . by day" refers to a difficulty or danger you are aware of, whether trouble with others, a business problem, or some other difficulty. The "terror by night" implies that there may be some complex in your subconscious or the existence of some dangers outside of yourself. You should use common sense and be alert and alive to all things going on around you. If someone is covertly working against you, pray frequently as follows: "There is nothing hidden that is not revealed to me. There is nothing covered that is not made known. I am surrounded by the sacred circle of God's love, and God watches over me." Read the 91st Psalm. It is the foremost Psalm of protection, and it will work wonders for you.

Nine in the fourth place: . . . *And when sailing was now dangerous . . . Paul admonished them* (Acts 27:9). In the journey of life, we may experience danger as we go by air, sea or land or on the street. Remain quiet and calm, do not fight the situation mentally. Use ordinary caution while at the same time knowing that God's love surrounds you, enfolds you and enwraps you. Realize that where you are God is and that "He careth for you." Trust the Divine guiding principle within you, and you will be led to move forward at the right time in the right way.

Six in the fifth place: . . *Clouds there are without water* (Jude 1:12). When clouds do not yield water to wash the earth, symbolically it means your meditations or prayers (clouds) yield no fruit or result. You can overcome this dry period in your life by realizing that the Infinite Intelligence in your subconscious knows the way out and that your faith in the Infinite powers within you will enable you to rise above all obstacles, and you will attract to you all those who will aid you in the realization of your particular assignment.

Six in the sixth place: . . . *Their glory shall fly away like a bird* . . . (Hosea 9:11). The bird means your thought life. The bird which flies off and does not return to earth for procreation, for food or to build its nest means your desire or idea has no resting place and no foundations under it. In others words, your desire or idea is not felt as true. It is not incorporated into your subconscious mind. Mental coercion and trying to force things and building castles in the air without any foundation under them lead to loss and frustration. Your ideals and aspirations must not remain "up in the air." They must be accepted as true and must be demonstrated in your life. You must demonstrate your faith in God and the good.

## 63. Chi Chi/After Completion

— —

——— **above K'an, The Abysmal, Water**

— —

———

— — **below Li, The Clinging, Fire**

———

*The Judgment*

. . . *But he that shall endure unto the end, the same shall be saved* (Mark 13:13). Persistence, stick-to-itiveness and determination to reach your goal will pay dividends. Do not rest on your laurels. Realize that eternal vigilance is the price of liberty. Likewise, there must be eternal vigilance by you over your thoughts and mental attitude. Keep alert and alive. Be on the *qui vive* at all times. Carelessness and inattention to your thought-life and imagery can lead to confusion and loss. Continue in right thinking and right feeling, and all will be well.

*The Image*

All of us are moving through the opposites in life such as night and day, ebb and flow, in and out, hot and cold, sickness and health, sweet and sour, hard and soft, love and hate, faith and fear, and male and female. All these are halves of the one whole. Going through life, the spiritual-minded man goes back to the center of harmony within himself and he reconciles the opposites. When fear or worry comes to your mind, go to the center of yourself and realize that God is all there is and God is Love and His Love goes before you to make straight, joyous and glorious your way. You have translated the opposite back to Spirit. Persevere in doing this and you will lead a charmed life. All is Spirit and the manifestation of Spirit. In reality one part of Spirit cannot be antagonistic to another part. Spirit is one and indivisible. Salute the Divinity in the other person.

*The Lines*

Nine at the bottom: *And be not conformed to this world: but be ye transformed by the renewing of your mind . . .* (Romans 12:2). The "world" means the mass mind, which is full of fear, anxiety, superstition and ignorance. Do not permit that type of mind to govern you. You must choose your own thoughts and your own direction in life. Avoid the contagion of the multitude. The crowd is always wrong. Go within yourself instead, and ask for God's guidance and claim Divine law and order is operating in your life; you will go forward then at the right time, and in the right way, and accomplish your aims.

Six in the second place: . . . *He that humbleth himself shall be exalted* (Luke 14:11). This is not a doormat attitude. On the contrary, it means a man who is conscious of his true worth and is humble enough to give all power to God within him and not to any man or organization. Realize that no one can demote you, hurt you or deprive you of your true place in life. Your workshop is your mind in tune with the Infinite, and your mental tools are your attitudes and choices. Choose true place, right action; feel, know and claim that you are always in your true place, doing what you love to do, Divinely happy and Divinely prospered. The law of your mind will confirm this and success is yours. Be humble before the law of your mind, which is: whatever you impress in your subconscious is also expressed.

Nine in the third place: . . . *Remember the covenant of their ancestors . . .* (Leviticus 26:45). The root meaning of "ancestor" is beginning. In the beginning God—this means the Life-Principle in you, which is called your Illustrious Ancestor in the *I Ching*, is our common Progenitor—the Father of all. The enemies are of your own mind, such as fear, hate, greed, covetousness. Prayer heals by destroying evil. Good thoughts are spiritual vibrations and possess much higher and finer vibrations than negative thoughts, which are of a much lower vibration. Prayer stops your mind from vibrating at a lower level. The devils that plague man's mind are fear ignorance and superstition. What becomes of all the negative thoughts when you contemplate the truths of God? They have ceased to exist. If you again indulge in fear, criticism, self-condemnation, looking upon others as inferior, and the like, you will get into trouble. Practice the Golden Rule and treat everybody as you would like to be treated. Then you will succeed and prosper.

Six in the fourth place: . . . *And drowsiness shall clothe a man with rags* (Proverbs 23:21). When man is asleep to the powers of God within himself, he becomes a victim of the mass mind with its jealousies, fears and intrigues, all of which mean rags. You should be clothed in the garments (mood, feeling) of faith, confidence, love and the song of triumph in your heart. The Bible says: . . . *Be ye therefore wise as serpents, and harmless as doves* (Matthew 10:16). Be discerning and perceptive enough to see what is going on. Be on the *qui vive*; be vigilant, astute and open to both inner guidance and counsel from without. Refuse to compromise with the truth. Play also the role of a dove, which is a symbol of purity and peace. Cremate and burn up all negation with the fire of Divine Love and faith in God.

Nine in the fifth place: *To what purpose is the multitude of your sacrifices unto me? saith the Lord: I am full of the burnt offerings of rams . . . and I delight not in the blood of bullocks, or of lambs, or of he goats* (Isaiah 1:11). A "sacrifice" in the *I Ching* and in our Bible is not depriving yourself of some needed good in order to satisfy a being other than yourself; the sacrifice you make is to give up negative and destructive thinking for constructive and harmonious thought-patterns. In other words, give up the lesser for the greater; for example, perform some act, such as a sacrifice hit in baseball. Oftentimes at sea, when a ship is in distress, it lightens its cargo in order to reach port. In all instances, to sacrifice means to give up your burdens of sickness, poverty and ill will, and to realize the abundant life. Many people practice rituals and ceremonies; they make pilgrimages, fast and follow all the tenets and rules of their churches and yet their lives are chaotic and tragic. All external activities are meaningless unless accompanied by a change of heart. It is what you really believe deep down in your heart (subconscious mind) that is made manifest; not what you theoretically give mental assent to.

Whatever your desire is—that is your offering, as you can't give God anything. Your desire is a gift of God. Affirm feelingly and knowingly: "God gave me this desire. I envelop it in love and I know it is sinking down into my subconscious now, and through the power of God it will come to pass." This represents the acceptance of God's gift, which is the real sacrifice.

Six in the sixth place: *Remember ye not the former things, neitner consider the things of old* (Isaiah 43:18). The past is dead. If your head is turned and looking backward, you can't go forward. It is foolish to linger over a pit into which you may have fallen, as though you enjoy the memory of an unpleasant experience. Be a true builder, waste no time in retrospection of old hurts and losses. Change your thought and keep it changed. Your future is your present thinking made manifest. To dwell on the negation of the past is to think about it now, and the past becomes your present thought. Inasmuch as your thought is creative, you are simply looking for trouble. Stop doing it and you will go forward.

## 64. Wei Chi/Before Completion

——<br>
— — **above Li, The Clinging, Flame**<br>
——<br>
— —<br>
—— **below K'an, The Abysmal, Water**<br>
— —

*The Judgment*

*Take us the foxes, the little foxes, that spoil the vines . . .* (Song of Solomon 2:15). The meaning of the root of the word "fox" in the

*I Ching* and in the Bible is burrower. A fox burrows a hole or tunnel in the ground. You must not permit fear, worry or doubt (foxes) to burrow into or hide in or even gain entrance into your mind, because if you entertain these foxes, they will spoil the vines—the good things of life. Fear, worry and doubt set up obstacles, difficulties and failures in your life. Begin to listen to the truth and affirm boldly: "God is my guide and my counselor. I have no fear, for God is with me. God is the only Presence and the only Power. I am now moving forward in Divine order at the right time and in the right way. I am at peace." When you are at peace and your confidence is restored, you can then move forward. To begin with fear is to end with failure. To begin with faith in God is to end in success.

### *The Image*

*In all thy ways acknowledge him, and he shall direct thy paths* (Proverbs 3:6). Before any journey or undertaking, be it what it may, always begin with God and assert feelingly and knowingly, "God is an ever present help. God is my guide and my strength, and God brings all things to pass in my life in Divine order through Divine love." Always go back to the center of your being where God dwells and listen to the voice of the Divine, and you will be inspired and succeed in harmonizing all things. You will bring to pass your heart's desire.

### *The Lines*

Six at the bottom: . . . *Behold, now is the accepted time; behold, now is the day of salvation* (II Corinthians 6:2). Salvation is the solution to your problem and is available now, for in the mind-principle there is no time or space. Time and space belong to this objective world you live in. Now is the accepted time for you to get your mind at peace, because when you are in a disturbed or a confused state of mind, whatever you do would be wrong. The beginning and the end are the same, and if your mind is in disarray and is chaotic now, it is the wrong time to advance. Read the 23rd Psalm; believe what it says. Get your mind in order and wait until you are at peace within before you act. When you begin with faith and confidence, your path will end in success. Get your mind in order now.

Nine in the second place: . . . *The trying of your faith worketh patience* (James 1:3). Do not be anxious. Anxiety is faith in the wrong thing. Haste makes waste. Have faith that you can accomplish all things through the God-Power which strengtheneth you. Go forward with that idea foremost in your mind. Be persistent and patient, knowing that all seeds come forth after their kind. Don't try to hurry the God-Power. Your attitude of mind will bring success and prosperity to you.

Six in the third place: *Thou wilt keep him in perfect peace whose mind is stayed on thee* . . . (Isaiah 26:3). Do not go forward or undertake any assignment until your mind is at peace. Whatever you start to do, the first step is to tune in on the Infinite One and have implicit faith that through the power of God you can accomplish, and you will succeed. When your mind is focussed on the Divine Presence within you, you are at peace, and peace is the power at the heart of God. Call on the Divine Power, which will respond to you. Also realize that Infinite Intelligence will attract those people to you who can aid and assist you in the realization of your heart's desire. You will reach your goal.

Nine in the fourth place: *God is my strength and power, and he maketh my way perfect* (II Samuel 22:33). Realize Divine love goes before you, making straight, easy and perfect your way. When fear, worry or obstacles come into your mind, supplant them at once and affirm, "I can do all things through the God-Power that strengtheneth me." No matter what the difficulties, doubts or impediments that seem to block you, keep on knowing that victory is yours. Look toward the joy of overcoming that which is set before you. The way opens up and you will receive rich rewards in many ways.

Six in the fifth place: *Both riches and honor come to thee, and thou reignest over all* . . . (I Chronicles 29:12). The riches of your mind consist of faith, confidence, assurance and wisdom. You are illumined from On High, and you are radiating love and goodwill to all. God's wealth flows to you freely, joyously and lovingly, and you are prospered spiritually, mentally and in all other ways.

Nine in the sixth place: . . . *These men are full of new wine* (Acts 2:13). "Wine" in the *I Ching* and in the Bible signifies joy and an exhilaration induced by the Spirit of God in the heart and mind of man. You feel inspired and God-intoxicated, which means the wine of joy, of success and of accomplishment. The feeling of joy is always experienced in the act of overcoming. Maintain balance and poise at all times. Realize that it is the joy of the Lord that always ensures your strength, your health and your security. With your eyes stayed on God, you will always maintain serenity and equilibrium. Make it a constant habit to drink of that old wine of heaven until the day breaks and all the shadows flee away.

# Get Published!

***"Everyone has something they know well or can do well. And when a person has a skill, there's always going to be someone willing to pay for it."***

***parkerpub.co***

Parker Publishing Company helps authors publish more titles. So whether you're writing a metaphysical, romance novel, a historical fiction, a mystery, action or suspense story, poetry, business, a children's book, or any other writer, we can help you reach your publishing goals.

Since 1960 we've offered a unique publishing experience to Authors, all over the world. Parker Publishing Company wants to help new authors in all aspects of publishing. The editing, marketing, multi-media design and copyright production and enforcement. From eBooks, Paperback, Hardcovers to Audiobooks can be produced in small volumes and offered to the public.

Besides telling a story, a book is a promotional tool. A book can be likened to a powerful business card since most people won't throw it out. Authoring a book can give you credibility and status, enabling you to charge more for your services.

Your writing will reach more than 20,000 retail accounts worldwide (chains, independents, specialty stores, and libraries). Our United States, Australia and United Kingdom-based sales teams work with clients all over the world through our broad distribution channel partners. For more information please contact us at **www.parkerpub.co**

PARKER
PUBLISHING COMPANY

**OTHER INSPIRATIONAL AND METAPHYSICAL BOOKS**

**FROM PARKER PUBLISHING COMPANY**

**THAT YOU WON'T WANT TO MISS!**

- Amazing Laws of Cosmic Mind Power, Joseph Murphy
- The cosmic Energizer: Miracle Power of the Universe, Joseph Murphy
- The Cosmic Power Within You, Joseph Murphy
- Helping Yourself with White Witchcraft, Al G. Manning
- Infinite Power for Richer Living, Joseph Murphy
- Life Beyond Life: The Evidence for Reincarnation, Hans Holzer
- Miracle Power for Infinite Riches, Joseph Murphy
- The Mystic Path to Cosmic Power, Vernon Howard
- The Power of Miracle Metaphysics, Robert B. Stone
- The Power of Your Subconscious Mind, Joseph Murphy
- Prosperity and the Healing Power of prayer, B. Turner
- Psychic Energy: How to Change the Desires into Realities, Joseph Weed

- Psychic Perception, Joseph Murphy
- Psychico-Pictography: The New Way to Use the Miracle Power of your Mind, Vernon Howard
- Secrets of the I-Ching, Joseph Murphy
- Secrets of Mental Magic, Vernon Howard
- Telecult Power: Amazing New Way to Psychic and Occult Wonders, Reese P. Dubin
- Wisdom of Your Subconscious Mind, John K. Williams
- Wisdon of the Mystic Masters, Joseph Weed
- Your Infinite Power to Be Rich, Joseph Murphy

BUY THEM AT

**www.parkerpub.co**

OR YOUR LOCAL BOOKSTORE

®PARKER
PUBLISHING COMPANY

9 789368 377764

Printed at Repro India Ltd.